"Florence Tsai is unusually wise. She is an expert in navigating tricky family dynamics across generations and cultures. What I love most about *Phoenix Rising* is the way it mixes historical case studies with her own experiences to ask the important question: How do you build something new while staying true to your legacy?"

James Cham
Bloomberg BETA

"Fabulous for families in business, politics, philanthropy, arts, and sciences. Read this book to survive another day in business—then another generation. Don't lose the untapped talent closest to you. That warning is the best part of this book, and you should heed it."

George Courtauld
Best-selling author of *The Pocket Book of Patriotism*

"Florence Tsai can really write! She employs a brisk snappy style—dare I say hip—to give us a fully referenced and intelligent analysis of what makes and breaks family enterprises. Written for both specialist and layman, Florence Tsai draws from ancient Greek and Asian mythology, studies on what makes healthy relationships, the complexity and richness of family dynamics, and even dares to bring in child development, all the while proving her point with case studies of particular business persons who either succeeded or failed or both.

She explains what enables families to be nourished by their predecessors and create a successful family enterprise. For those interested in family enterprises (who isn't?) but also for the philosopher, economist, and historian, Florence Tsai's *Phoenix Rising* provides telling insights into how capitalism really works, how it adapts, innovates, disrupts, and continues to survive in ways both surprising and exciting. I do wish someone like Karl Marx or Joseph Schumpeter could have had the chance to read it."

Nick Papandreou
Brookings Global Leadership Council economist,
Secretary of the Andreas Papandreou Foundation,
author of *A Crowded Heart, Mikos and Manos* and
The Magical Path to the Acropolis,
and screenwriter of "Little Greek Godfather"

"In *Phoenix Rising*, Florence Tsai offers a new model with frameworks that advance the study of business longevity. Institutions are always looking for new insights, but business lessons often don't translate well across sectors. The long-run horizons of multigenerational family-run enterprises turn out to be surprisingly similar. Who knew? I was inspired by the remarkable families whose stories of renewal appear in the book. Institutions grappling with disruption can learn to develop exceptional and resilient new "Phoenix" leaders, experiment more, and make keep-or-kill decisions quicker by following Florence's "core and edge" strategy. This book opens up new and timely discussions for leaders of all types of organizations that want to spark innovation and thrive for the next hundred years."

Pareena G. Lawrence
President of Hollins University

"Florence Tsai has worked with family organizations from founders to next gens, and *Phoenix Rising* offers both the weight to convince and the tools to inspire. Florence's proposal for building and sustaining a legacy mindset ensures that leadership and innovation will remain the key focus for growth and longevity. An essential read for all family enterprises!"

Molly McAdams
Founder of Introducing Leaders and CEO
of Strategic Legacy Ventures

"This is a must read for any family business organization with aims to thrive in future generations. An essential road map providing the secret sauce to building generational family and business success. Great insights for inspiring, developing, and engaging next generation leaders."

Mike Hill
President and CEO of Minot's Light and member
of the Bancroft business family

"A valuable read! Great inspiration for your life's journey in business. Lots of tips on how to develop all the talent you've got, so you can build value for all to share. For over 60 years and across three generations, that's still what motivates me as chairman of a family business. My own journey began by working with my mom and my dad's brother, Bill … then with my wife, our four sons, and Bill's three sons … and soon (I hope) with many more from the fourth generation. Read this book and remember: give your rising leaders many chances to shine, back up your innovators, and don't let them slip away. Then, when you get to my stage, you'll look back on your career and realize, it's not all about the money you made or the successes you racked up, but the great people you had the good fortune to work with along the way."

Jack Mitchell
Chairman of Mitchells Stores and WSJ best-selling author of
Hug Your Customers, Hug Your People,
and *Selling the Hug Your Customers Way*

"This is a book that ushers in a new mindset, and a new direction for family business. Family enterprise has a perhaps undeserved reputation for lack of creativity. This book reveals the day-to-day, entrepreneurial energy of family business. It begins with stories from the past and present, written like no other business book I've read, in the style of the new millennial generation. It looks at how family business can become a 'quantum machine' for innovative growth and development. The core of the book covers the human life cycle, from childhood to elderhood, for insights on developing entrepreneurial focus, energy, and results in family business. It's full of stories of the creative energy of family and how it gets unleashed. You will never look at family enterprise the same way again after you read this."

Dennis Jaffe, PhD
Author of *Working with Those You Love,*
Research Fellow at Wise Counsel Research and
co-author of *Cross Culture*

"Florence Tsai is an amazing resource for large families looking to take a longer-term vision on their legacy, family business, and working with all family members. Guiding a large family through small and big changes takes patience, time, and resources. While many put emphasis on short-term gain and monetary reward, Florence shows in *Phoenix Rising* that experience, guidance, mentorship, and immersion in the new economy are what puts families on track for long-term success."

Brian Koo
Founder of Formation Group

With great energy and multiple examples from human nature, Florence Tsai builds a compelling picture of what makes 21st Century family enterprises thrive. She draws from famous stories ancient and modern, outlining the core characteristics of entrepreneurs who survived failure, coped with setbacks, and created businesses despite significant adversity. Phoenix Rising is a welcome addition to the growing literature on family enterprise development.

James Grubman, PhD
Author of *Strangers in Paradise:*
How Families Adapt to Change Across Generations

Phoenix Rising – Leadership + Innovation in the New Economy

Lessons in Long Term Thinking from Global Family Enterprises

Phoenix Rising – Leadership + Innovation in the New Economy

Lessons in Long Term Thinking from Global Family Enterprises

By

Florence C. Tsai
Founder, Center for Enterprising Families

Routledge
Taylor & Francis Group

A PRODUCTIVITY PRESS BOOK

First edition published in 2019
by Routledge/Productivity Press
52 Vanderbilt Avenue, 11th Floor New York, NY 10017

2 Park Square, Milton Park, Abingdon, Oxon OX14 4RN, UK

© 2019 by Florence C. Tsai
Routledge/Productivity Press is an imprint of Taylor & Francis Group, an Informa business

No claim to original U.S. Government works

Printed on acid-free paper

International Standard Book Number-13: 978-1-138-34668-0 (Hardback)
International Standard Book Number-13: 978-0-429-43719-9 (eBook)

Library of Congress Cataloging-in-Publication Data

Names: Tsai, Florence C., author.
Title: Phoenix rising : leadership + innovation in the new economy : lessons in long-term thinking from global family enterprises / Florence C. Tsai.
Description: 1 Edition. | New York : Routledge, [2019]
Identifiers: LCCN 2018055432 (print) | LCCN 2019006295 (ebook) | ISBN 9780429437199 (e-Book) | ISBN 9781138346680 (hardback : alk. paper)
Subjects: LCSH: Small business--Technological innovations. | Leadership. | Intergenerational relations.
Classification: LCC HD2341 (ebook) | LCC HD2341 .T733 2019 (print) | DDC 658.4/092--dc23
LC record available at https://lccn.loc.gov/2018055432

Visit the Taylor & Francis Web site at
http://www.taylorandfrancis.com

Visit the Center for Enterprising Families website at http://www.centerprising.org

To S.A.B. and all rising innovators

Contents

Preface   *xv*

Acknowledgments   *xxiii*

About the Author   *xxv*

1 *Part A* Family + The Quantum Machine
   (Chapter 1 for the Hackers). 1
   It's Imperative to Transform. 2
   Gods, Monsters, and Longevity DNA 3
   Future-Forward: Alexandre Birman and Arezzo 4
      Organizations designed for innovators 5
   Distributed Systems Are Fuzzier. 6
   The Quantum Machine. 8
   American Phoenix, A Hero's Journey. 9
      E.I. du Pont and the quantum machine 10
   Conclusion 19

1 *Part B* Family + The Quantum Machine
   (Chapter 1 for the Master Architects) 21
   The Evolution of Family Organizations 21
   Stage One: The Family Business 22
   Stage Two: The Family Enterprise. 25
   Stage Three: The Family Ecosphere 30
   The Quantum Machine Defined 35
   Centerprise—Build and Fire Up That Machine! 36
   The Five Arrows of the Rothschild Family 39
   The Evolution of Governance. 41
   Concentric Circles of Influence 42
   Conclusion 43

2 Longevity DNA 45
   Leadership and Innovation Culture at Corning 45
   Amo Houghton's Longevity DNA. 48

The Edge and the Core 49
British Theater's Quantum Machine...................... 49
Future-Forward Thinkers and Experimenters 52
Sinkhole Becomes Museum Piece: The Practical Futurist.... 53
The Four Capitals....................................... 55
Driving Your Quantum Machine with the Four Capitals 59
Conclusion 61

3 Phoenix Rising: Traits of Exceptional Leadership 63
The Centerprising Leadership Traits You Want
and Need... 64
Leadership Challenges Today 64
   Mandate to lead.................................. 65
   Governance roles................................. 66
   Versatility and cultural sensitivity 67
Leaders You Need 68
   Performance versus success......................... 70
Centerpriser: Portrait of an Effective Family Organization
Leader 72
How to Be an Exceptional Leader 73
How to Measure a Leader 74
Conclusion 75

4 Survival Hacks: Resolving Generational Tensions.......... 77
Tension One: To Fail or Not to Fail? 78
Tension Two: "I Need to Be Me" 79
Tension Three: Internal Drive—Can the Monster
Be Awakened? 79
Tension Four: Set Aside Your Internal Dictator............. 81
Tension Five: Finding Common Ground with
Millennials 82
Tension Six: Whose Vision Will Win Out? 83
The Secret to Resolving the Six "Tensions" 84
Spotting the Stars..................................... 84
Welcome to Your Second Career 85
Survival Hacks....................................... 86
Conclusion 87

5 Switch on the Longevity Gene........................... 89
Develop Leaders from the Moment They Are Born......... 90
   Secure attachment................................. 91

Forming a strong moral core 92
Parental engagement is imperative. 92
The "Rising Generation's Burden" 93
Waiting for the Marshmallows 95
Work Ethic and the Growth Mindset 96
What Kind of Person Is Your Child? 97
Early Childhood Is the Perfect Time to Learn Core
Values 98
Conclusion 100

6 Be Trustable to Teens. 101
Heading off Trouble at the Pass. 103
Concrete Strategies for Proactive Parenting. 104
Spend time with your teen. 104
Help your teen build a trusted friendship circle 104
Show up 105
Teens Must Choose a Tribe. 106
Building a Circle of Trusted Advisors 107
Keeping It Real with Your Teen. 107
Having the Money Talk with Your Teen 109
What Does "The Best School" Really Mean? 113
Stoking the Fires in Passionate Teens 114
Conclusion 116

7 Fast Tracking Your Almost Phoenixes 117
Young Adults Want Independence—But Engagement Too 118
Three Types of Wealth Creators 119
The Mindset of Wealth Creators 121
Profile of an Intrapreneur. 122
The insider 122
The explorer 124
Profile of an Entrepreneur 125
Profile of a Portfolio Builder. 127
How to Incubate Your Rising Leaders 128
Harness Their Passion. 130
Conclusion 131

8 Getting to Yes with Thirty-Somethings 133
The Clash Between Elders and Successors. 134
Making a Successful Entry. 136
Flexible roles for wealth creators. 136

How high can I reach? 136
How to get compensation right. 137
Wealth Creators and the Equity Upside. 139
An Abundance of Wealth Creators Ready to Lead at
Rothschild. 140
"Only An Owner" 142
Conclusion 144

 9 Frictionless Gearing for Quantum Impact. 145
How to Stay Aligned and Future-Focused 145
A Tale of Three Newspapers 146
Why Slow to Adapt? 149
Share the Vision or Lose It 151
You Can Ride the Waves of Disruption 152
Building Your Authentic Brand Culture. 153
Adaptation for Wealth Creators of All Kinds 155
Conclusion 156

10 Spotting the Stars. 157

Notes   163

Index   175

Preface

Do not pray for an easy life. Pray for the strength to endure a difficult one.[1]

Bruce Lee

This book is about the next chapter for some of the world's hardiest economic organisms: business families. In particular, the ones that thrive from generation to generation and share benefits with people in their interlinked ecosphere. Tech titans of the New Digital Age are starting to take notice of these business families' survival skills. For centuries, from East to West and North to South, these masters of longevity have been innovating their way through a scary world, just like the one we're facing today.

The family, as a global institution, tends to be risk averse. The institutions built by the tech titans, epitomized by the acronym FANG (Facebook, Amazon, Netflix, Google), tend to push the boundaries too far. They are proud of pushing the envelope to see what happens. So, families and FANG approach risk from opposite ends of the spectrum. Families can learn to experiment more, and to keep or kill projects quicker. FANG can learn to think more deeply about the ramifications of innovation, and they can also learn to be more responsive to feedback from society. The time is now for families and FANG to start working together more closely for mutual benefit.

The world keeps changing faster and faster. There are no do-overs for technology disruptions. We can't un-innovate. There's no un-learning genetic sequencing, for example, to limit the potential for designer babies. Some of the implications are stark, rushing at us with frightening speed, posing ethics issues that are beyond the horizon of our innovators.

Our beliefs about how humans live together, work together, and coexist with different cultures are also changing. We hardly had time to adjust to globalism before corresponding backlash brought on geo-political instability. Everyone's questioning everything, and it's difficult to get our bearings as business leaders. Is long-term growth better than short-term profit taking? Is it right or wrong to allow hate speech and fake news on social media in the name of free speech?

In the face of these dizzying changes, it's easy to forget that this isn't the first time in human history that our world is being transformed by quantum technology advancement. The more things change, the more they stay the same. There were technology revolutions in prehistory. There were several in the pre-modern era. Three industrial revolutions preceded our own fourth industrial revolution (4IR) era today. How did we adapt before? How did we guide the trajectory of quantum technology advancement? We did it with long-term thinking and an emphasis on survival over short-term growth explosions.

It turns out that both of these attributes are coded into the DNA of enterprising families that withstood upheaval and outlasted periods of disruption in their businesses, in their countries, and on their continents. A study of family enterprise serves as an ideal example for any non-family organization eager to learn how to thrive long-term, when the organization is characterized by key stakeholders who share the same values and mission. If we want to extract the lessons from family enterprise success, it's the culture of the families themselves and their innovators, not their products or their famous companies, that we should pay attention to.

Reid Hoffman, co-founder of LinkedIn, calls family companies "Phoenixes,"[2] recalling the long-lived bird of Greek mythology that regenerates in cycles of rebirth, nourished by the ashes of its predecessor. East Asian philosophy reveres its own mythological bird, Fenghuang, as a symbol of prosperity and happiness, built on the foundation of virtue, duty, propriety, credibility, and mercy. So it's no wonder that Hoffman admires Phoenix companies for their unique ability to rise and fall and rise again for one hundred years or more. But it's the *family leaders* behind those companies who are the real heroes. They are Phoenixes made of flesh and blood, not logos or brands or bricks and mortar. It's the family leaders behind Phoenix companies who are the master navigators.

Phoenixes are real people—talented, resilient individuals who rise at crossroads. They know how to renew and transform their way out of legacy businesses in sunset industries into fast-growing industries. Phoenixes see business strategy not in terms of months, but decades. They're equipped with a long-term lens that works like an explorer's telescope. Standing squarely in the here-and-now, they can zoom in on the future and navigate the hazards. Think of Phoenixes as commanders of a mothership during a storm. Like the seafaring Odysseus bound to the mast, they hear the sweet seduction of the tech sirens without succumbing to the destructive fate of the shipwreck afterwards.

Phoenix leadership serves families and their companies by riding out the storms of industry life cycles, knowing when to bet or fold at plum moments. Phoenixes do make mistakes and suffer failures. But they know they're heading in the right direction as long as the cumulative wins far exceed the collective losses.

John Elkann is an Italian Phoenix. His family's flagship business, Fiat, was under great financial distress as he stepped in to fill the shoes of his legendary grandfather Gianni Agnelli. Elkann says, "I learnt not to be desperate in bad times, and am learning not to be bullish when times are good."[3] David René de Rothschild is a well-known French Phoenix. He rebuilt his storied family's banking business from scratch when Banque Rothschild was nationalized in 1982, following the election of President Francois Mitterand. He woke up the next morning and got to work rebuilding. Rothschild reported feeling transformed. "I used to be an inheritor," he told Francois Mitterand, "and now I am a founder."[4]

That's an elegant way of saying that if you have long-term thinking in your DNA, you can use it for fuel to fire up your rising Phoenix, and it will guide you in judging what actions you should take in the short term. Longevity DNA can be acquired over long, intentional, meditational practice. But why not learn from enterprising families, where this mentality is second nature?

Look around the globe, and you will see that family businesses still thriving in the third generation or beyond are rare birds. They didn't succumb to the Three Generation Curse. Most cultures have a superstitious saying for it: "Wealth does not pass three generations." "*Fu bu guo san dai.*" "Shirtsleeves to shirtsleeves in three generations." The family business graveyard is littered with shooting stars that only cared about short-term profit, like Parmalat in Italy.

Survivors know they have to shift their mindset pretty radically—from problem-solving in "family business" mode to embracing the more complicated and holistic work of a *family enterprise*. They know they must ultimately build an interdependent ecosphere, or else they won't survive long. In the *family ecosphere*, doing good and doing well do not require tradeoffs. Long-lived enterprises last because of their social enterprise and their stake-holder engagement, not in spite of it. Interdependence with the world around you is adaptive and net positive. It may come as a surprise, but family businesses that are obsessed with profit alone will tend not to achieve sustainability. They won't be able to build a long-term, highly trusted family brand like Levi Strauss or Bechtel, Hermès or Henckel.

Now, imagine for a moment that you're head of a big, pub-licly listed company that is often criticized by shareholders for shortsighted focus on profits. You walk into a Pilates class. You've brought your friend, the seasoned business executive. You're both out of shape. You barely know where to start working out. And then you see that the class is full of super fit students of all ages, work-ing on their core strength—or to be more precise, on their moral core development in the business, because this class is designed for enterprise fitness. The other students range in age from four to ninety-four. They explain that they've built organizations in every country on earth, and they're happy to take you through the core training routine. They have a lot of experience. Counting their own parents, who brought them to this class, they've been doing Pilates for one hundred years or more. They look healthy, strong, centered, and anchored. They train hard. They had the foresight to make room for you on the floor. They want to know what you can teach them. Who are these people?

They're families. Enterprising families.

This is a business book about the regenerative power of enter-prising families to give rise to the exceptional family leaders that we call Phoenixes. You'll learn how they can renew their busi-nesses, their families, their communities, and activities they engage in while strengthening a moral core and nurturing values that become defining characteristics. It's a book about the wisdom of being an exemplary family member, company, or business leader on the path to long-term sustainability, not one who focuses too much on wealth or power.

The winner-take-all mentality is not giving rise to the excep-tional leaders we need in large organizations. That mentality is successful in the short term and benefits society by evolving econo-mies and industries. But the sustainability of the winner-take all mentality is coming into question. Thus far, it has institutionalized disruption by building lumbering, tone-deaf monopolies. They wield enormous power, whether by giving voice to people around the world and supporting their livelihoods, or refusing service by kicking them off their platforms and cutting off the umbilical cord to their communities.

Pushback from stakeholders in the gig economy of our millennial-centered digital world is inevitable. And conflict comes to a head whenever the tech titans don't respect their stakeholders as value creators. The millennial stakeholders of FANG are, after all, participating both as consumers and workers. They may be a highly fragmented and segmented global population, but they know how to amplify their voices with technology. The tech titans need to earn their respect. If the tech titans want to thrive in this fourth industrial revolution, and not get disrupted by social institutions, they'll need the mandate from stakeholders to lead people, not just companies.

The problems of leadership and governance facing the tech titans may make their companies more vulnerable to sudden death. Around the world, industries are changing so fast that legal frameworks and governments can't keep up. Facebook and others have yet to accept the consequences of the natural power that comes with the technology they have introduced. It's not yet clear, for example, how they will participate in global governance of fake news. A new era of self-regulation is dawning for business leaders and shareholders, where there is an imperative to do the right thing—not because we're forced to do it by law or profit, but for long-term survival and because it is the right thing to do. Can FANG be trusted to self-regulate?

Companies need to take responsibility for proactively influencing the evolution of governing frameworks for the benefit of those they lead. That's a geeky way of saying that faceless companies and business leaders need to build a moral core. Only then will communities follow their leadership. Only then will people support their businesses.

Enduring family enterprise has an inherent advantage that can be widely deployed to disrupt tech titans, if necessary, in meeting these universal, growing problems. That advantage is long-term thinking. Having endured beyond life cycles from birth to death and rebirth of the industries, political states, and social institutions on which they pinned their financial fortunes, family enterprises intuitively understand that a strong moral code equals survival. That's why the starting point of unifying any business family for multi-generational success is to craft an expression of the values, mission, and vision you share.

But it isn't enough to possess an inherent advantage. It needs to be set in motion right away, at ground zero wherever the enterprise needs to keep up with the new economy pace, otherwise there won't even be time for the nimblest family players to set up a viable strategic position to capture value. If they take this immediate action, they will also be leading their old economy industries by persuasion and a strong moral core.

This book encourages tech titans and innovative Phoenixes to work togther for mutual benefit. It should also serve as an alarm bell for the owners and leaders of family companies around the world. If your family hasn't evolved yet, from a singular focus on the existing business (or businesses) to broader engagement of all your family talent in the larger family enterprise of shared activities, then you're really behind. You're in danger of succumbing to the Three Generation Curse. And that's not all. There's another curse: the Curse of Dichotomous Outcomes. Family enterprises, on average, either perform much better than their non-family competitors, or else they perform much worse. We'll talk more about that monster later in this book. It's a curse that haunts family businesses (and their rising leaders) who are not performing significantly above average. If that sounds like you, this book is your wake-up call.

Thriving in the New Digital Age requires a family enterprise to rapidly transform its mentality, culture, and identity. It requires a new tool-kit for surviving and thriving—even for the stars in the family business world. This book shows how that can be done.

For general business readers who are interested in innovation, leadership, social enterprise, strategy, and shared value, I'm presenting insights about the evolution of family enterprise and its newest strategies. Most readers will have some experience with family enterprise themselves, and I've written the book for you. I hope it will arm you with the wisdom, agility, and purpose that leads to bringing forth a Phoenix or two in our fast-changing world.

If you're a seasoned leader of successful organizations, this book will teach you how to evaluate your possibilities in this New Digital Age, so you can take action to ride the wave instead of being crushed by it.

If you're a rising leader, you'll learn how to communicate better with your elders about the New Digital Age and the roles you can play. This will integrate the two worlds (old economy and new economy; their world and your world) harmoniously into your life. You'll feel calm moving between both worlds, no longer plagued by the doomed sense of being forced to choose between them. You'll learn how to gear into the large ecosphere that the senior leaders steward, tap into their renewable resources, and introduce disruptive thinking to ignite the remodeling of your family enterprise.

Soon, I hope, both generations will be working together more effectively and having more fun charting your route and transforming your ecosphere.

This book also offers some new strategies for working globally. More than 80% of the challenges that family companies face are shared by them all, no matter where they are in the world. This key conclusion was reached decades ago by my mentor John Davis from Harvard Business School, whose research pioneered the academic study of family business management. Despite differences in culture and socio-political-economic structures, family companies the world over exhibit far more similarities than differences. Their core DNA shares the enterprising spirit, even though their bloodlines are distinct. There will always be people who choose to profit from highlighting differences and creating conflicts, rather than spotlighting commonalities and promoting harmony.

There's currently much talk, for example, about the difference between the U.S. and China, about whether democracy and autocracy are governance systems equally capable of nourishing a thriving population.[5] What gets lost in the debate is how essentially similar family enterprises have thrived and created great prosperity for economies in both countries, thanks to enterprising individuals and families. Non state-owned, private companies founded by entrepreneurs in China make up at least two-thirds of the nation's GDP.[6] This book will discuss how the DNA of both Eastern and Western cultures in successful family businesses makes their renewal and transformation possible.

Because of their commonalities, the strategies deployed by enterprising families across the globe are very similar. Those that embrace the principles and practices of Phoenix Rising renewal learn that when they engage people (inside and outside the family) to develop all four kinds of capital (financial, social, human, and intellectual), they can place themselves at the center of the concentric circles of influence that they build. Around them, they gather tech disrupters, social enterprise innovators, and cultural change agents who get pulled into the family's orbit and integrated as resources the family can use beneficially to make meaningful investments for people to thrive. I call this work "centerprising."

Through centerprising, families create talent force fields that become foundations of their new wealth engines.

Just as there will always be readers who emphasize differences over commonalities, there will always be critics of capitalism who object to building wealth of any kind. As income inequality and wealth gaps widen all over the world, this sensitivity is something I can understand. Let me be clear about what wealth means to me and how it is treated in this book.

This book doesn't lionize companies, families, or business leaders who prioritize wealth or power. It doesn't equate wealth with excess consumption. Instead, it equates wealth with the opportunity to do good and make investments for people to thrive. Wealth and power can be very positive tools when they are wielded with benevolent intentions. This book challenges you to measure success by how creative, resourceful, and innovative you and your organization can become. It encourages you to embrace change while staying committed to the long-term, multigenerational success of your people—in whatever you aspire to.

I hope, after reading this book, you'll dedicate yourself to making meaningful investments for people to thrive. I hope these stories and lessons give you the courage to take bold action from a strong core of authenticity, rather than risk oblivion. Succeed, and one day you'll see your Phoenix Rising.

Florence C. Tsai
Newton, Massachusetts

Acknowledgments

I would like to thank the following people:

To my good friend and colleague Suzanne Stroh, for her invaluable contributions in writing this book. She generously shared her life journey and experience growing up in a multigenerational business family. I'm inspired by her insights and tireless efforts to continuously improve the probability of success from generation to generation. Her entrepreneurial spirit further confirms my belief that family enterprise is one of the best vehicles for achieving long-term, shared value in business ecospheres globally.

To Harvard and MIT Professor John A. Davis, my mentor in the family business field, for introducing me to the world of family enterprise, its positive influence, and its potential to create positive impact in the world. I count myself among the lucky few who can say, of their professional development, that they learned the ropes from a pioneer.

To Anand P. Raman, for his counsel on developing this book. Anand's expertise as editor-at-large at Harvard Business Review Group helped me focus on what general business readers worlwide can learn from family enterprise.

To the enterprising families I have worked with, for committing to sustainability of their shared resources far beyond their own lifetimes, and for showing me that people are the game-changers to bet on for the future.

To the team at Routledge/Productivity Press, for being so great to work with.

And, finally, to my family, my trusted anchor in all of life's challenges, for their love and unwavering support in whatever I do.

About the Author

Florence C. Tsai is a business strategist with broad industry expertise. She advises chairpersons and CEOs in the Americas and Asia, with a focus on the world's leading family companies. Co-author of *Built for generations,* the UBS Family Office Compass (Zurich: UBS/CIFE 2016), Florence has designed curriculum and lectured at family enterprise education programs held at the Harvard Law School and private banks. She speaks at the World Economic Forum Annual Meeting of the New Champions in China.

A pianist from the age of three, Florence studied under Master Teacher Dorothy Hwang at the Colburn School in Los Angeles. She holds an A.B. in Economics from Harvard College, an M.P.A from Harvard Kennedy School of Government, and an M.B.A from Harvard Business School.

Florence Tsai is Founder and Managing Director of the Center for Enterprising Families (http://centerprising.org) that incorporates disruptive technology and long-term thinking to spark innovation and achieve sustainable family enterprise transformations. She lives with her family in Newton, Massachusetts.

Family + The Quantum Machine (Chapter 1 for the Hackers)

If you can't ride the wave and transform, you'll be crushed by it.

Nothing says quantum like "Iron Man."[1]

Have you seen the Marvel movie starring Robert Downey, Jr., Terence Howard, and Gwyneth Paltrow? If not: spoiler alert!

Before there was Iron Man, there was Tony Stark. Let's take a look at the week that changed the life of a rising leader at Stark Industries.

We're in a Humvee cruising across the Afghan desert. The fashion-forward California tech titan looks a bit out of place here, with a glass of whiskey in hand, trash-talking his U.S. military security team. Meet twenty-something Tony Stark aboard the mothership, cocky after a successful, mega-million-dollar sales meeting. Son of a legendary weapons developer, Tony built his first circuit board at age four, his first engine at age six, was a rock star at MIT, and became CEO of Stark Industries at twenty-one, on the death of his father Howard Stark, the founder. Tony is talented and he performs above average. He knows it and he shows it.

Suddenly the convoy comes under fire. The unit takes heavy casualties. Tony's on his own. Fleeing the scene, he's injured in an explosion, loses consciousness, and is taken prisoner in a network of mountain caves. Tony's fellow captive, Ho Yinsen, performs surgery to save Tony's life. Tony regains his senses with an electromagnet embedded in his chest. Connected to a car battery, the crude device is the only thing keeping shrapnel from entering his heart. But Tony calculates it won't last long. He knows he's a dead man walking.

Under torture, Tony agrees to build a next-generation Jericho rocket from the Stark Industries technology that his captors have stockpiled. In despair, Tony doesn't even want to get started. He reasons that he and Yinsen will only be executed anyway. Yinsen confronts Tony with his time horizon. Tony admits that he's only got one week to live.

"I guess it's a pretty important week, then," observes Yinsen.

Now determined to survive, Tony fights back. He and Yinsen work around the clock to design and build a powerful electric generator out of palladium scavenged from Stark Industries components. It will be enough to power his heart for fifty lifetimes... "or run something big for fifteen minutes," Stark hints to Yinsen. We realize the men are planning their escape.

So, fifteen minutes will decide their fate. If successful, Tony will have a very long horizon. His heart will never grow old.

Tony adapts his design from the large Arc Reactor built by his father. To save their lives, he lets Yinsen embed the next-generation Arc Reactor in his heart.

Now it's a race against time to make use of the iron and other materials on hand to stage their escape before Tony and Yinsen's betrayal is discovered.

I'll stop here, so you can enjoy the film as much as I did. It's enough to say that Tony Stark's innovation is what I call a Quantum Machine. The Arc Reactor is a force multiplier of every asset Tony can deploy. It's a Steampunk concept, integrating industrial age materials with digital age technology. Its impact is far greater than the value of any of its component parts—including Tony's own life, since he and Yinsen face certain death unless he innovates.

And there's one more reason why I'm telling you this story. The skills and assets Tony used to build the Arc Reactor were passed down from his dad.

It's Imperative to Transform

The secret to longevity is the ability to transform. Change is inevitable. And in some time periods, like now, the pace of change is very fast. So, change is inevitable, but transformation is not. Transformation is intentional. If you or your organization can't ride the wave and transform, you won't be able to get in front of it. And you'll be crushed.

The most talented rising leaders will not shine, create, or innovate if they just slide into the suit that senior leaders designed or laid out for them to wear. Rising leaders need to go through their own struggles, learn how to fail, and rise from the abyss to become robust leaders who gain from disorder, as described by Nassim Nicholas Taleb, the scholar and risk analyst who coined the term "antifragile" to describe this property in resilient systems.[2]

Make no mistake about failure, it's a hard fall. Failure feels like getting smashed into pieces. Building yourself back up is brutal rehab. What senior leaders and other elders on the mothership can do, besides protecting rising leaders from core-shattering danger, is to give them the tools, teach them the skills, and lend them the compass from the family's treasure chest of core values to maximize the rising leaders' chance of success.

But rising leaders should choose their own environments and fight their own battles. That environment could be the existing family company. Or it could be a start-up, or investing for the family office, or founding a social enterprise, or taking a demanding job outside the family business, or even serving in the military. Inside or outside the family enterprise, the proving ground for rising leaders needs to be one of their own choosing. All rising leaders, especially Phoenixes, need to be the explorers and pilots of their own lives. Sammy Lee, from Hong Kong's venerable oyster sauce company Lee Kum Kee (LKK), is such a Phoenix. We'll meet him later in this book. He started a health products company in China to diversify the family's business portfolio. Sammy Lee's startup went through difficult times as most businesses inevitably do, which almost broke the family apart. Did this story end well? You'll find out later.

Gods, Monsters, and Longevity DNA

Back in the age of gods and monsters, Hercules was tested with twelve labors. It took ten years for Odysseus to find his way home. During the struggles every rising leader faces, what's being put to the test are the core values passed down from the family. Those values that are deeply internalized will be activated regularly in meeting challenges. Those that don't fit the circumstances will stay "switched off," like inactive DNA. With growing self-awareness, the rising leader learns to recognize those useful core values and their benefits. Then to strengthen them with new vigor.

By this time, after battling a few monsters, it's clear that the rising leader has internalized the parts of family DNA that he or she thinks can help them survive and thrive, like Iron Man, who used the Stark DNA to survive, then adapted it for pursuing his own True North of doing good.

Hercules' labors finally came to an end, and Odysseus eventually returned to Ithaca. The rising leader brings the reconstituted family DNA back to the mothership with new resources to guide the whole family enterprise through a transformative renewal process. There are added benefits, besides entrepreneurial success, when senior leaders at the core anchor rising leaders who gravitate toward the edge. Successful innovators always work with collaborators. What you want is for them to bring home those collaborators who can strengthen the core. They can help you build the know-how and confidence to launch another entrepreneurial venture. It's a virtuous cycle that you can reinforce, with the proper gearing, to create a force field that continuously sucks fertile resources back into the center. This is the work of what I call centerprising, and it's how the family enterprise evolves in ways that enable it to survive and thrive over generations.

If family companies and their fully-tested leaders can link together in meaningful ways with the tech titans of the New Digital Age, there can be enormous benefits for society. People trust family enterprise leaders. A 2014 Edelman global survey of more than 20,000 executives and "general public" respondents found that family companies and their leaders are more trusted than non-family companies, their leaders, or leaders of any other social institution.[3] That's a branding opportunity worth aiming for. So, how do you develop trusted leaders? You let them test themselves.

Encouraging rising leaders to test themselves, to battle their monsters, is the mechanism for perpetuating the Longevity DNA that gives family enterprise its enduring advantage and accounts for multigenerational success. Spot and develop trusted leaders in the family enterprise, and your organization stands a good chance that it will be more trusted and have more moral authority for generations to come.

Future-Forward: Alexandre Birman and Arezzo

Alexandre Birman, from Brazil, loves designing shoes, like his father. As a boy, he was a hard worker, always ahead of the curve. As a young teen, he made a deal with his family to convert unused property into a parking lot that he operated after school. He managed four employees and bought his first car with the profits. At fifteen, Alexandre left school for Italy (where he lived in lodgings and didn't even speak the language) to learn shoemaking from the world's best craftsmen. He discovered a real talent for styling women's shoes, which grew into an all-consuming passion.

So why did Alexandre walk away from his father's company, Arezzo, in his early twenties to start his own shoe company? He felt creatively and financially blocked by conflicts with senior managers. On his own, with a $3 million loan from his father, Alexandre designed and marketed his first collection of high-end shoes. The line took off with a distribution deal from a major retailer in New York. For the next decade, Alexandre built Schutz into a brand with worldwide recognition. In 2007, the brand was doing so well that CEO Anderson Birman invited his son to merge their two companies into a footwear powerhouse.[4] It's a good example of the quantum effects of investing in a rising leader who isn't just thinking ahead, but throwing himself headlong into the future. Leaders like Alexandre Birman have what I call Future-Forward mindsets, combined with Longevity DNA, that the world needs more of today.

Many business families would consider a move like Alexandre's, from the core out to the edge, to be highly risky, both for the family enterprise and for a rising leader who has been traditionally "groomed" to take over the existing business. If that's also your assessment, I hope this book will change your mind. It is never "risky" to develop an entrepreneur; it is a necessity. The entrepreneur is not likely to change his or her type. One secret to Arezzo's success is the relationship between Alexandre and his father, Anderson Birman. Alexandre was lucky to have a very attentive father who was convinced that backing the fashion startup was the right path, given his son's strong entrepreneurial drive. With the founder-father's unwavering support and strong connection, the Phoenix was able to move confidently out to the edge, and willingly back to the center, after proven success. The beauty of centerprising is that this way, family talent can more easily move back and forth between the edge and core without your losing them.

Organizations designed for innovators

To understand why Arezzo is the exception in family business, and not the rule, let's take a look at what has shaped the popular wisdom so far.

Until now, the field of family business studies has focused primarily on the business organization. The goal was protecting the "goose that lays the golden egg." Business families seeking expert advice on best practices learned to define and manage the drivers of the organization's success. So, the role of family talent and its importance have been mainly viewed from the perspective of how they drive the organization's success. If there's no role for certain specific family talents in this schematic, little attention is paid to developing them, and they get marginalized. Marginalized talent can have breakout potential; but too often, people who have been sidelined don't have high levels of engagement with the family business organization. And the reason is because the center of gravity has traditionally stayed in the current operating businesses. Arezzo found a way to engage family talent outside the core business.

And there's another factor that makes Arezzo a rare success story of its kind. If your company does spark innovation in an outlying venture, it's much rarer, but sometimes wiser, to fold the successful entrepreneur back into your core operations. But this requires the co-existence of two very different cultures in the same organization. How many organizations will rise to that challenge? And so Arezzo's success remains, unfortunately, an outlier in the world of family business. Many breakout successes in business families never make it back to the core.

But it doesn't need to be that way. There's a new way to change your traditional management culture to a Future-Forward innovation culture. It's happening more and more. Later in this book, you'll read about the transformation of the Danish family business, Vestergaard, from apparel manufacturer to medical products developer and social enterpriser when the rising leader invented LifeStraw.

The prevalent way of thinking about family business used to be, "organizations before innovators." It's little wonder that family business has been conceptualized this way by the experts. Their theories worked in the past because their models mirrored the way other successful, highly stable business organizations were structured. The IBMs, GEs, Samsungs and other blue chips of the world operated with hierarchies, clear chains of command, clear and timely reporting, and clear organizational boundaries. Innovation was orchestrated from the core in large R&D departments. You could almost judge their efficiencies (thus their profits) by their organizational charts.

Those days are over. What now?

Distributed Systems Are Fuzzier

Even when examining many of the great, top-down, non-family business organizations, family business experts had already noticed evidence of a quality that makes family business so unique:

the emphasis on fairness as a defining cultural characteristic. John Davis likes to joke, a baby's first word is "Mommy." Next comes, "That's not fair!"

Familes tend to emphasize fairness and flatter organizations. This happens because family organizations, by nature, tend to be more distributed. They're held together by common identities and shared cultural norms. They share values, vision, and a mission, and they own financially lucrative assets together for shared benefit. And, most importantly, families govern their organizations primarily by persuasion, with a few guiding principles that act like golden rules or rules of thumb.

Family owners are very different from owners or shareholders of other organizations. Driven by an unshakable commitment to mutual survival, family owners are Future-Forward by definition. They are highly motivated to stay together as an ownership group. That team spirit creates expectations. Business families expect financial benefit. And they are willing to invest in a sheltering social environment that gives the sense of belonging and offers comforts under stress. Once they have made the commitment for their enterprise to outlast them, family owners are motivated by more than just personal financial gain. To them, ownership carries a lifelong sense of purpose.

In the early 21st century, the 5th and 6th generation *New York Times* family owners stayed together through a financially challenging period to transform their newspaper and sail it into the digital age. Their business survival was at stake; it was innovate or perish. *Wired* magazine described the company as "clawing their way into the future."[5] During their struggle, the Ochs-Sulzberger clan watched every major competitor go bankrupt or sell out to other industry titans.

Looking on as the newspaper industry's financial value was being eroded daily in the marketplace must have been frightening for the family, whose wealth is tied up with the company, but they stood steadfast in their commitment to publish America's newspaper of record. They took this stand not primarily out of financial motives, but because they share a belief in independent news reporting "free from fear or favor" as an organ of democracy that they are responsible for protecting. Like Iron Man, the New York Times hacked its survival using its Longevity DNA.

Contrast that survival strategy to that of a similar non-family company, where shareholders are bound together by an opportunity to collaborate—but only as dictated by economics—to achieve financial gain in the short term. The two companies may look similar, but their responses to stress won't be the same.

In the New Digital Age, companies are moving fast to a distributed organizational system. The term "distributed system" comes from computer-speak. It refers to any number of independent computers that are powered separately and linked by a network. In a distributed system, organizational boundaries are fuzzier than in the top-down organizations of the old economy. There are fewer full-time employees accountable to the chain of command in the hierarchy. There are more part-time employees. Many people involved in business operations aren't even employees; they're independent collaborators or joint venture partners. And unlike in the past, where many part-time employees had clearly-defined, regular, and reliable work schedules, the sharing economy (also called the gig economy) has delivered a "just in time," part-time workforce that functions as needed to fill demand. Today, many if not most workers at every level of expertise can choose when and how much they want to work. In this new reality, companies are transforming their organizations from hierarchies to networks.[6]

To succeed in this New Digital Age, family organizations need to mirror their distributed counterparts. Family businesses already have some experience with this, because it is innate to their experience of running families multigenerationally. They're late to catch up with the rush from "old economy" organizational structures to "new economy" ones, but they should be able to master the transformation if they adopt a Future-Forward mindset and follow the program I outline in this book.

The Quantum Machine

To cope with the realities of the New Digital Age, it's now critical for enterprising families to adapt, innovate, and evolve quickly into a family ecosphere with fuzzier boundaries and a more distributed network of wealth creation engines. The next part of this chapter will explain what a family ecosphere is, and how it operates, in detail. For now, here's the big takeaway: to evolve, you've got to shift your focus away from organizations to the individual rising leaders in your family. Think about how the family organizations can support each family member as precious talent. Your new measure of success should be the number of family members your family enterprise can spot, develop into leaders, launch, and maintain active engagement with.

I know, it's easier said than done!

But you can do this and reap the benefits if you only learn to think, like a mantra, "Family + the Quantum Machine." What's a Quantum Machine? It's the secret weapon on every hero's journey.

American Phoenix, A Hero's Journey

This is the story of an American Phoenix who emigrated from France, got the attention of Thomas Jefferson, and built a gunpowder factory that changed the world. His true story is like the real-life Steampunk version of Iron Man—with an extra twist: Eleuthère Irénéé du Pont de Nemours was the founder of a family ecosphere you can still visit today, where he built a Quantum Machine that has played a key role in American history.

He was an immigrant, with Alexander Hamilton as his lawyer, but this isn't a rags to riches story. He gambled everything, but he wasn't a risk taker. He was a technology innovator, but he wasn't an entrepreneur. E.I. du Pont was an intrapreneur. Have you ever heard of that term? It's an entrepreneur working inside the family enterprise, with family resources. There will be more about the importance of spotting and developing intrapreneurs later in this book.

We've already met one: Tony Stark. Iron Man is a superhero intrapreneur who's tailor-made for the New Digital Age. He learns by "standing on the shoulders of giants" like Howard Stark. Tony's grateful for getting a leg up in life, but he doesn't take it for granted. He's got one foot in the past and one foot in the future. His innovations promise mega-scale solutions to problems that seem intractable—even species-threatening. His armored suit, good enough even when forged from Iron Age materials, reminds us that humankind has age-old skills that have protected us for millennia from threatening new technologies we don't understand. It gives us hope for a better world in an era of chaos and upheaval.

Two hundred years ago, around 1800, the world was in a similar place. The Industrial Revolution had started half a century earlier, with boom money from the British victory in the Seven Years' War. Invention of the mechanical spinning wheel and the steam engine brought factories and railroads to England and Scotland, making Britain the center of the industrial world. Like today, the new technology had crossed a frontier, and there was no going back. The world never went back to hand-sewn shoes, never went back to coal mining with hand buckets, never went back to pony carts from locomotives. There was huge economic growth. Talented designers from all over Europe gathered in London to pitch their new technology "efficiency machines" to the "venture capitals" of the day. Everybody was getting funded.

Then came the American and French Revolutions, followed by the Napoleonic Wars. These disruptions checked the dominance of Great Britain and halted the spread of technological progress to France and the U.S. Venture capital dried up, innovations stalled, and business prospects didn't seem as good as they were before.

While all this was shaping up into a perfect storm, imagine being a French entrepreneur and politician like Pierre Samuel du Pont de Nemours, who had invented laissez-faire economics. You now had governments changing like musical chairs. You had already been imprisoned twice. The first time, your execution literally got rescheduled for Robespierre, when you were lucky enough to escape. The second time, you got sentenced to hard time for life on a penal colony; again, you got lucky when a powerful influencer, Madame de Staël, intervened before they shipped you out. If your business career in France looked uncertain to you, it was almost paralyzing for your two sons, Victor (a charming diplomat) and Irénée (a failed chemist working in the family publishing house).[7]

Our story continues with Pierre's younger son, Eleuthère Irénée du Pont. Before things could get better for Irénée (prounounced EAR-ray-nay) and his family, they were about to get worse. Much worse.

E.I. du Pont and the quantum machine

There had been two successive generations of strong, practical, and educated Huguenot women in the family when Irénée du Pont was born in 1771. He was the second son.

As we have seen, Irénée's father, Pierre, was a political economist, a poet, and a prominent figure of the French Enlightenment, alongside Voltaire. As a boy, Pierre's father Samuel du Pont had been a stern man, a fine watchmaker who had brought his business to Paris from Rouen in 1735, then set up shop in the rue Harlay. Samuel had been so threatened by his son's intelligence that he banned his wife from educating Pierre. But she was headstrong, and Samuel's tactic backfired. Pierre avidly studied military science and technology before ultimately turning his back on the family watch business. Before walking away from his father forever, Pierre wanted to prove himself to the patriarch. He wanted his father to know that he had inherited the family DNA for watchmaking. So, he built a magnificent timepiece, said to be the envy of every craftsman in Europe. Out of spite, Pierre inscribed it in Greek, which he knew his father couldn't read. When the work was finished, he presented it to his father. They exchanged sharp words. Pierre walked away. And as far as we know, Pierre du Pont never spoke to his father Samuel again.

Pierre might have pursued a career in military technology. But his experiences had turned him into a pacifist. So, he turned to poetry and political economy. Voltaire liked his poetry, but other people told Pierre to stick to economic analysis. Writing important papers at twenty-three, "du Pont anticipated by some thirteen years Adam Smith's basic thesis that money is not wealth, and by over a century Henry George's advocacy of a single tax on land."[8] Today he's considered the father of laissez-faire ("laissons-nous") economics. In the 1770s, Thomas Jefferson and Benjamin Franklin were among his readers.[9] Pierre du Pont became Inspector General of Commerce under Louis XVI in 1774. He would become one of the king's closest, most trusted advisors.

So, E.I. du Pont had a highly social luminary for a father, the kind that consulted other luminaries for a baby name. The du Ponts named their boy Eleuthère for "free" (from the Greek Eleftherios) and Irénée for "peace" (from the Greek Irene). The irony was written in the stars, as you'll see, because life was neither peaceful nor free for Irénée from the start.

He was a quiet, introspective boy strongly influenced by his mother, as Pierre had been by his own mother, a driven woman from a noble but impoverished Huguenot family who had died young. Pierre du Pont considered his son Irénée dull but hardworking. He preferred his eldest son, Victor, and made no secret of it.[10] The irony was that Pierre and Irénée shared a couple of important things in common. Neither was graced with beauty. And both were fascinated by machines and their workings. I'll leave it for you to decide how closely this bonded father and son.

Irénée and his brother Victor embarked on their adolescent journeys as the sons of a great man. Irénée shied from the limelight, but

Victor enjoyed it. Whereas Victor pursued diplomacy and became secretary to the French consulate in New York, then later the French consul in Charleston, South Carolina, Irénée didn't seem very motivated. He studied chemistry and took a job at the national powder works under Lavoisier, the famous chemist, but quit as soon as Lavoisier moved on. Irénée was content, after that, to work as a printer in his father's new publishing house—financed with a loan from Lavoisier.

Irénée had been thirteen when his mother died in 1784. The death of Irénée's mother happened only months after the king granted the du Ponts a title, de Nemours, and coat of arms with the motto "Upright I stand." There was a fateful scene. Pierre du Pont adored his wife, even though he had been mostly an absentee husband. Her death must have triggered painful memories of losing his own mother, who had been his bulwark against a disapproving father. Somewhat self-consciously, but also out of real grief, Pierre gathered his sons and told them to swear a unity pledge to one another.[11] Irénée made this pledge faithfully, which was also to have a great impact on his life.

Pierre barely survived the French Revolution when, in 1789, after being elected a member of the new Estates General from Nemours, he decided (despite being a pacifist) to help the royal family escape Versailles by staging a diversion at the Tuileries. The bloody battle killed nearly all his friends; Pierre du Pont was one of only six who survived by stealing a red cap and slipping into the crowd. He went into hiding, fled the city, and somehow the monarchist escaped the guillotine during the September massacre.

Irénée, meanwhile, had become a revolutionary. In 1791, he defied his father by marrying the woman he loved, Sophie Madeleine Dalmas, who had none of the desirable social connections to fulfill Pierre's aspirations. Sophie turned out to be a faithful companion and an excellent manager of family resources. She was another strong woman in the family tradition, and eventually won over her father-in-law. Sophie was one of the only people the taciturn Irénée ever confided in. The couple had three children who survived these turbulent years. Irénée's brother Victor, the diplomat, married a high-born woman overseas, and the Victor du Ponts began raising their children as Franco-Americans.

Even though Pierre's social capital was strong enough to weather the death of his last powerful patron, the king's mistress Madame de Pompadour, Pierre's political situation was precarious, and in 1797 the business was raided when one of Pierre's publications was suppressed. Irénee was dragged off the printing press and jailed with his father. They got out of jail within a week, and Pierre was never sent to the penal colony, but they felt their life was in danger and quickly started making plans to emigrate. Together with Victor, they formed a company, Du Pont de Nemours Père et Fils & Cie, and started looking for investors in the real estate development business. Pierre's plan was to build an "old economy" farming community in Virginia.

Pierre already had quantum returns in mind, and anyone who has ever made a start-up pitch will recognize their own first draft in the prospectus that promised:

> No danger, no risk of loss of capital … the certainty of drawing interest—first at four percent, then at six, then at eight; and finally after twelve years, the certainty of capital that has been quadrupled, probably increased tenfold, possibly even twice tenfold.[12]

When Talleyrand, the foreign minister, backed the prospectus, Pierre was able to raise FF450,000 francs. But that was only about a tenth of the FF4 million he was looking for. It would be barely enough money, Pierre caluclated, to buy high quality farmland in the U.S.[13] But they had to risk it. Pierre sold all his assets except his country house. He converted Lavoisier's debt into equity in the new company, and the du Ponts took the plunge.

Nobody died on the Atlantic crossing, but it was a harrowing journey. Formerly a fugitive from the law whose choices had led to his son's imprisonment, Pierre's role as a protector was now reaffirmed. Sophie's mettle was tested as well, in keeping the family together with dwindling resources aboard ship, and this was the journey that won her universal respect as the family matriarch.

The large family landed in Rhode Island, where they were welcomed by a letter from Thomas Jefferson. Victor and Pierre settled in New York, keen on deploying their capital right away. A year passed, and after making direct investments in seven sophisticated projects, over a broad range of traditional business activity, none seemed to be panning out. They weren't getting anywhere.

Irénée was a hardworking type who never gave the impression of being an idler, but the reality was that he'd been given little to do. He was bored. One day, Irénée accepted an invitation to go hunting with a fellow Frenchman, Louis Toussard, now a colonel in the U.S. Army, who had settled in a farm in Delaware near Wilmington. They ran out of gunpowder and stopped at a country store to resupply. Irénée was shocked by the high price and low quality of the ammunition. When Toussard explained that the only reliable powder was a British export, widely unavailable to locals in every state, Irénée was intrigued. He inspected a gunpowder plant in Pennsylvania and found the whole operation appallingly inefficient. His training as a chemist was enough for him to see that the saltpeter was poorly refined and the graining was bad, producing none of the uniformity that was the key factor that made black powder a reliable explosive. He decided to go into gunpowder manufacture. "So Irénée had returned home with Project No. 8 to add to his father's and Victor's list. Pierre Samuel did not at first greet Irénée's proposal with much enthusiasm." For one thing, Pierre and Victor were snobs. They looked down on gunpowder production as an unglamorous, blue-collar, industrial business where low profit was only rewarded with high danger.[14]

Now Project No. 8 wasn't going anywhere, either.

Irénée saw excitement where the others only saw a deadly grind. Irénée could also see the business opportunity in gunpowder as explosives for clearing land for farming. Thomas Jefferson liked that idea.[15] Armed with the great man's approval, Irénée went back to his father and declared, defiantly, that he would build the factory himself. He drew up a plan, calling for $36,000 in capital, and asked his father and his brother for funds to start his "black powder" mill. He argued that nobody could deny that he was a hard worker (which was true), and that even an unattractive opportunity could flourish with hard work. Maybe not the sexiest of pitches.

Pierre and Victor promised to invest $22,000 from the family business after Irénée raised $14,000.

Little did Irénée know, on returning to Paris to seek investors, that his greatest weakness would yield one of his enduring advantages. Irénée's problem was, he had no charm. He was still able to make use of his father's charming country house, but the subtleties of social interactions had to be listed among his liabilities. Luckily,

Irénée understood this about himself. So Irénée decided that his best calling card would be to get expert validation of his plan by somebody (or something) with high authority.

He chose the military for his sponsor. He'd worked at the national gunpowder factory as a chemistry student. He could approach them "with his first name, not his last," as the French saying goes. He decided to ask the French military for technical advice—and, hopefully, access to new technology. To do that, he had to convince the military that if they helped him on his journey, they'd be working in the country's best interest. So Irénée made the fateful decision to incorporate his American business as a French company: E.I. du Pont de Nemours & Cie.

It worked. Irénée got the meetings he asked for. To his surprise, he learned that French commanders knew all about the gunpowder supply problems in the U.S. Whereas the British strategy of exporting black powder across the Atlantic protected their trade secrets and IP (intellectual capital), it left the British gunpowder manufacturers vulnerable to tariffs or even an embargo. Working directly with Irénée could gain the French military a future customer in a market they knew would literally explode, since France and Britain were hovering on the brink of a war that they knew would, without a doubt, be fought in the New World. Working with Irénée would give French investors access to a new market poised for huge growth. And since Irénée would manufacture in the U.S., there was no risk of tariffs or embargos.

The French military gave him everything he needed, and Irénée returned to America with skilled labor, machinery, and plans for a factory that would employ cutting edge hydraulic technology— but barely enough capital to get started. With the $6,000 raised in France, he began scouting locations up and down the Eastern Seaboard, even without the matching funds from his family.

On the western banks of Brandywine Creek in Delaware, not far from Toussard's farm, two healthy cypress trees stood beside the still waters of Hagley mill pond. Planted to celebrate a marriage, the trees were already one hundred years old when Irénée, Sophie, and their family arrived in 1801. It was a good omen, and they decided to build their factory on the site, with a house nearby. Purchasing that land—making that commitment, "staking the land"—was what it took to secure the business partner he needed. Now the money fell into place.

Nobody in America had seen anything like the factory Irénée du Pont intended to build. The plans must have looked like Tony Stark's design for the Arc Reactor. Irénée had chosen this site for a very specific reason. The Brandywine is not a major river, but it strikes a vein of extremely hard, blue, igneous gabbro rock. Irénée needed that stone. His design called for a "powder yard" of several strange, bunker-like, heavily reinforced, trapezoidal stone structures he would build for grinding black powder. The structures had to be rock-stable, because all the timber supports would have to be joined, not nailed. (No metals—not a single nail—could be used in construction of the entire factory, for fear that a spark would start a fire that could create an explosive and deadly chain reaction.)

He also knew he'd need to dredge, expand, and line every inch of the existing Hagley mill pond and its millraces, plus install water gates, to secure a water source that could deliver steady, renewable power for the volume of production he planned. He needed hard, non-permeable stone for that—stone that could be quarried locally. Like the Brandywine blue gneiss.

So, crews of carpenters, ditch-diggers and masons were assembled along with their families, housed, and put to work. Labor costs were higher in America. On top of that, a competitor tried to dam the creek upstream, which would have forced Irénée to acquire the land. Instead, he hired one of the country's top lawyers, Alexander Hamilton, to negotiate a purchase of water rights, then tore down half the dam.

Irénée soon realized that the existing water wheel wasn't producing enough water power. He needed heavier iron grinders to produce more of the finer granules that he knew would revolutionize the industry. Massive grinders would require more power, and handling such volatile materials under higher pressure would also make the work much more dangerous. A single spark could blow up the entire factory. Power delivery would have to be uniform, consistent, and reliable. So, with the help of the pioneering engineers he'd brought from France, plus collaborators he'd met on his scouting trips, du Pont started working on a design for a new kind of waterwheel aptly called the "Hecules" turbine.

This gave the old mill pond new, important status. Uniform pressure could now be maintained on a more efficient waterwheel to deliver more power but avoid disruptions in power that could create deadly sparks. Another innovation was needed.

So, they lined the eight-foot deep mill pond by hand with gabbro, block by block, so it would protect their most valuable, renewable resource: the water, taken from the river, needed to run the machinery safely and reliably.

Now they started forging the machinery they needed out of iron, including steel tracks for railway carts, massive grinders, waterworks, and a system of gears, wheels, leather belts, and iron shafts that Irénée envisioned would drive power from one water mill to sorting machines and several grinders.

Irénée's costs were skyrocketing out of control.

To raise more money, Irénée was forced to take out a bank loan. He even loaned his shares to a local partner, but managed to maintain sole control of the company.

At this point, Irénée didn't even technically "own" a single piece of his own business. Meanwhile, in New York, Pierre and Victor weren't having any luck with any of their seven projects. E.I. du Pont could easily have lost everything even before Eleutherian Mills was ever built.

And he didn't even have a single order yet. Irénée's relationship with his local partner was souring. The partner wanted a higher stake in the business for promoting it.[16] They soon resorted to legal battles, distracting Irénée further.

Luckily, Thomas Jefferson came through with Irénée's first order for 22,000 pounds of gunpowder. It would be used, not for clearing fields, but in a Naval war against the Barbary Pirates. They had been threatening the Caribbean rum and sugar trade that American ships had been protecting, at good profits, for the mutual benefit of French, British, and Dutch merchants. Why, exactly, did Jefferson help secure the first order? You will find out in Chapter 2.

Starting black powder production, Irénée du Pont began the next leg of his journey. Think of the quantum effect of the water in that mill pond when, in 1804, he installed the cutting-edge Hercules water turbine and turned the wheel that opened the water gate. Water came flooding through the millrace over the turbine, powering iron machinery that was among the first of its kind in America. It was a very high tech, high performance, "new economy" system making use of a low tech, renewable resource protected and replenished by the family.

The ability for a family leader to drive the family's renewable resources—for the du Pont family, it was water; today it is family talent—into an engine (or turbine) that can generate massive power is the first aspect to think about when building your own Quantum Machine like the one in the family ecosphere at Eleutherian Mills, the home and the enterprise of the du Pont family.

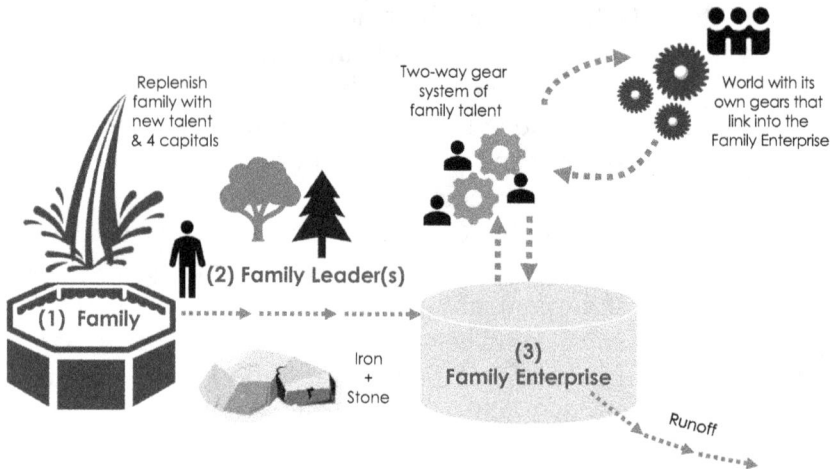

Family + The Quantum Machine. (Florence C. Tsai, 2018)

Now harnessing more power from the same source, Irénée added new ways to direct that power from the turbine and convert it for gaining advantages in speed or torque. He did this by making use of a simple, effective gear system to drive and control that power. This is the next thing to look for in your own Quantum Machine design. How many organizations and links does your family enterprise organization need (think of them as gears, shafts, levers, and belts) to drive power where you need it?

Irénée's millraces could now safely turn several giant, eight-ton iron grinders in several bunkers of the Powder Yard at Eleutherian Mills. The mass production of gunpowder stabilized the community with high-paying (if dangerous) jobs and transformed the American industrial landscape almost overnight. This is the kind of power you can create when you set your family enterprise in motion. This is the force multiplier effect that you're looking for when designing your own Quantum Machine. The value of your output for many stakeholders (consider that there was no black powder of similar quality anywhere in the country at the time) far outweighs the costs.

But at Eleutherian Mills, as in many start-ups, the quantum earnings effects weren't seen immediately. Revenue at the end of

1804 was $10,000 for 45,000 pounds of powder—only double the revenue that Irénée thought he could produce before installing the turbine. Good, but not great.

At the same time, Pierre's and Victor's losses in Projects No. 1–7 were so steep that they filed bankruptcy the next year, in 1805. Irénée swallowed the parent company and assumed all its debts, also taking on financial responsibility for his father and Victor's household. Victor moved his family down to Delaware and built a house across the river, on the east bank of the Brandywine—well out of range!

Irénée was still burdened under heavy financial obligations, but cash flow was rising steadily on strong sales, based on the high quality demonstrated in product tests. Sales were $43,000 in 1807.

Eleutherian black powder proved to be stable, precision-ground, uniform, and now widely available, finally delivering the volume of controlled explosions required by arms manufacturers eager to roll out a new generation of weaponry. Du Pont's innovation would have no equal until Alfred Nobel invented dynamite in 1863.

In 1807, the embargo foreseen by the French military finally happened. President Thomas Jefferson placed a ban on foreign gunpowder, cutting off British supply. Sensing that war might be imminent, Irénée reinvested all profits from the gunpowder mill to keep up with demand. Then, during the war of 1812, production jumped to half a million pounds of powder for sales of $143,000.[17] And it kept going up exponentially from there for the rest of the century.

Hagley and Eleutherian Mills on the Brandywine, the du Pont home and the family enterprise, with its water gates, mill races, turbines, and two-way gear system, served as a living family ecosphere for several generations and gave rise to one of the world's giant chemical companies. In 2017, Du Pont merged with rival Dow Chemical. In 2019, Du Pont will be restored when Dow Du Pont splits into three separate companies.[18] In the meantime, Hagley is a family ecosphere that has been frozen in time and perfectly preserved. You can still visit it today.

Better yet, build your own!

Conclusion

The du Pont family business made a quantum leap that day by the mill pond in 1804 when it installed the Hercules turbine. To make quantum leaps in your own family enterprise, turning it into an ecosystem that produces Phoenixes in one or more of your linked gears, you need what E.I. du Pont and his family built in the ecosphere at Eleutherian Mills, their home and their enterprise. You need to set your family enterprise in motion and build a Quantum Machine.

> **Are you curious about Quantum Machines that other families have built? Would you like to meet other cool Phoenixes? Visit centerprising.org.**

Family + The Quantum Machine (Chapter 1 for the Master Architects)

Centerprise everyone on the team to transform each player into a Phoenix.

Seasoned leader, do you often feel that next generation members, even members of your own family, are not on your same team? It's like they think you don't think right, dress right, talk cool, work impactfully? Where did these people come from? They don't even speak your language. Do they sometimes seem like space invaders? Is that why they're obsessed with Mars?

Believe it or not, these Martians may look green, but when it comes to outlasting the competition and doing good while doing good business, they actually have your DNA. They just express it differently. You ride the DeLorean time machine from "Back to the Future,"[1] and they ride the Batmobile from "The Dark Knight Trilogy."[2] But both revolutionary modes of transportation get you there using powerful technologies that harness many forces under your control and multiply your impact for good work.

So, if you can't look past the green skin of those destined to follow you, you really are missing out!

To understand rising leaders' view of the world and how they envision doing good while doing good business, let's take a look at the evolution of family organizations.

The Evolution of Family Organizations

The family is a highly stable social institution. When families organize themselves to own assets together and to conduct business or engage in politics, education, science, social enterprise (whether for profit or not for profit), religion, or the arts as a family, those organizations tend to look and act pretty much the same, all over the world.

What's more, they tend to evolve in predictable ways over time. Until now, experts only recognized two evolutionary stages. I now see evidence that a third stage of evolution is taking place—and needs to take place—around the world.

So, let's take a closer look, starting with the family business, since profit-making production of goods or services—or else engaging in trade—are usually the first building blocks in any family enterprise.

Stage One: The Family Business

A family business is a profit-making enterprise intended to support the family, where two or more family members have ownership today, or where plans have been made for a founder to pass ownership to one or more family members. The family business is composed of owners, family members, and business employees.

Mortality is high. The Three Generation Curse means that by the third generation, less than 15% of all family businesses will still exist. There are several potential causes, including industry decline and family conflict. Looking at financial performance alone, studies done by John Davis and myself, based on historical performance of the Forbes 400, show that multigenerational family companies have dichotomous outcomes.[3] Compared to non-family company peers, the family business will either perform markedly better—or much worse. The family company tends not to sit in the middle and be average. This is the Curse of Dichotomous Outcomes.

The reason for this big spread in performance is that family companies in general depend on strong family leadership. They place less reliance on a professional management team. What does it take to outperform the non-family competition? You need unity in the family. You need family talent for innovation. You need good stewards. And you need a sound, clear family wealth strategy. If you don't have all four of those things, your family business is likely to crumble.[4] Shared assets get divided and the result is a smaller financial base. As a result, the family loses access to attractive investment opportunities. It's a downward spiral from there.

Back in the 1970s my mentor, John Davis—then a PhD student at Harvard Business School, where he would go on to become Senior Lecturer—began conducting field research on family businesses with his own mentor, Harvard social psychologist Renato Taguiri.[5]

In 1978 they published a major breakthrough in a working paper summarizing their field research. They had developed a simple model that gives a comprehensive explanation of the nature of family companies. Extremely elegant, the Three-Circle Model is still in daily use today around the world, primarily as a tool in succession planning.

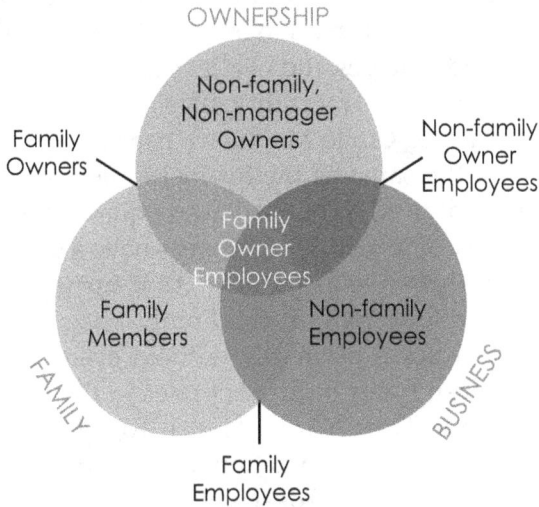

OWNERSHIP

Non-family,
Non-manager
Owners

Family
Owners

Non-family
Owner
Employees

Family
Owner
Employees

Family
Members

Non-family
Employees

FAMILY

BUSINESS

Family
Employees

The Three-Circle Model. (Tagiuri and Davis, 1982)

Three-Circle structures are as old as Celtic runes and Russian wedding rings. Today we're so familiar with the concept above, it's easy to forget that it was never used in business at all before Davis and Tagiuri introduced it for family business. They made an important contribution.

Imagine how huge it was to visualize, for the first time, the way that such a complex form of enterprise was structured for stability and endurance over long periods of time. How reassuring and calming to realize that the structure itself was simple—not complex. As it turns out, most of the complexity you need to manage in family business is due to overlapping roles, the conflicts they create, and the decision-making problems that result.

Suddenly, the Three-Circle Model made it easy for everyone in the family to see the three major organizations that make up the family business system. They could place themselves in the model as family members, owners, and employees.

Lightbulbs started going off for business families that wanted to battle the curses and outlast their competition. Using the Three-Circle Model as your framework, it becomes clear that every stakeholder in the family business system has a different set of perspectives and interests. Some interests are naturally aligned, while other interests are naturally in conflict. For example, family owner-managers share the same desire as non-family employees to reinvest in the business. However, unlike non-family employees, they also benefit from dividends paid to owners. Dynamics like this give rise to the innate advantages and challenges of the family company that we see contributing to mortality rates.

Through the Three-Circle Model, we can also see that the family mission is not the same as the business mission. Owners have their own goals that need to be respected equally. Leaders need to respect boundaries. Non-family employees have a place at the table. So do spouses in their role as parents. As it turns out, everybody of any age has a role to play in the family business system, and the system can't perform optimally without everyone doing their part. There are seven types of distinct roles in the family business system, based on the Three-Circle Model. Together, they form the unique family business organization that, statistically, has high potential to outperform or self-destruct.

With this model as a tool, friction points could be logically identified—even anticipated—and addressed. Individuals playing more than one role could now clearly see where their roles overlapped, causing conflicts that needed to be managed. At the center with the most complex role are the owner, family member, and business leaders with control who needs to balance the interests of all three circles.

That person is almost always under a lifetime of stress, trying to keep it all going and running smoothly. Luckily, other leaders emerge as needed. For all leaders and their followers, the Three-Circle Model can pinpoint responsibility for making important decisions. That increases accountability for leaders to make timely decisions. Almost as importantly, people in the family business system were relieved to find that others in the family, in the ownership group, and in the business could now "see them" and see where they stood in their role on any issue. Their perspective and unique contributions would no longer go unnoticed or underappreciated. The Three-Circle Model supercharged many enterprising families and turned family members into team players in high-functioning systems with better odds for survival.

For decades, the Three-Circle Model has been useful for aligning interest groups, especially in finding and training a successor for the existing family business. If you have ever worked on improving your family business system, you know that the focus is on developing one person, or a core group of family members, as leaders—with other family members providing support and oversight. The Three-Circle Model is a useful training tool for building decisiveness. It helps with short-term planning and developing medium term strategy. But more is needed.

In succession planning today, the problem is this. Change is now accelerating so fast, it's hard to know how business will be changing in five years—let alone ten. So what criteria should be used to spot and develop the right family successor to take over the existing family business when your end goal is a moving target? Will the family business still be controlled or even owned by the family in ten years? Will it be sold? Or shuttered by the unforgiving forces of sunset industries? There were signs in the early 2000s that for an increasing number of families, the Three-Circle Model does not address all their problems.

And what about the problems of multigenerational families that share assets but conduct primary activities together other than business—like the Rockefellers, Pritzkers, Annenbergs, and many other household names in American philanthropy?[6] Or the Oppenheimers, Phippses, or Burdens (members of the Vanderbilt family), who pioneered the modern family office for making investments? Or the Bushes in the U.S., the Papandreous in Greece, and others who have now produced two, three, or more generations of political leaders? Those activities, accomplishments, and resources aren't accounted for in the Three-Circle Model, where the center of gravity is focused on the family business leader and his or her problem of how to perpetuate the current operating companies and/or other financial assets.

Stage Two: The Family Enterprise

After much debate over what was foundational to multigenerational success, John Davis's model of the family enterprise has gained wide acceptance globally.

A family enterprise is defined as an organization that is the collection of all assets and activities that family owners share. It is structured as a group of independent, but interrelated, organizations that collaborate and, ideally, coordinate with each other. In the diagram below, the organizations look like the petals on a flower.

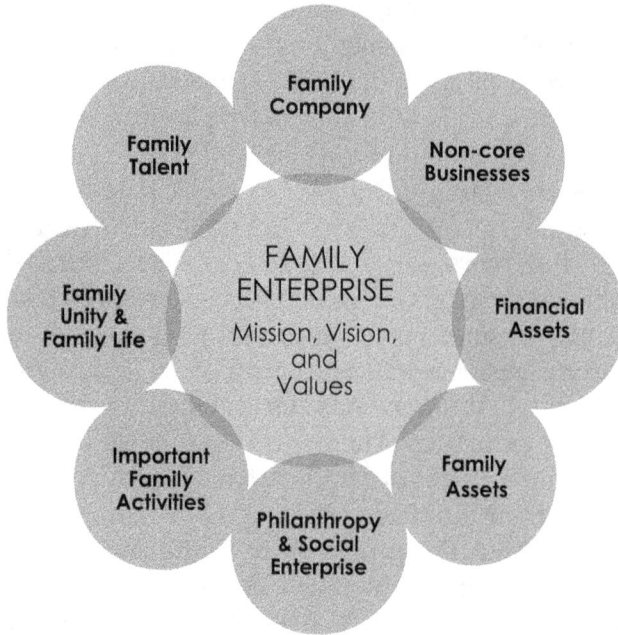

The Family Enterprise Model. (John A. Davis, 2013)

At the core of the Family Enterprise Model is the group of engaged family members who create governance structures based on shared family values, mission, and vision to operate the organization. This set of articulated statements at the core serves as the guiding principles for family and non-family members working within each petal entity. The core governance structure brings unity of purpose to the overall family enterprise.

Each petal entity can contain one or more activities shared by family members. The organizations can be formal, like companies or foundations, or informal, like committees or projects in incubation.

This model is, essentially, a screenshot of the family enterprise at any given time. Family organizations can use the Family Enterprise Model to: (1) identify all the family's shared assets and activities; (2) map the flow of information among them; (3) coordinate among them; and (4) develop talent specifically for each petal entity.

The Stage Two model shows us that the family endeavor has changed in an important way. The center of control at the family business stage was the family business leader(s) with controlling ownership. Examples are company founders and family business leaders controlling the family's primary wealth engine, such as Bill Ford at Ford Motor Company. Now, in the family enterprise stage, what's at the center is an organization consisting of a group of actively engaged family members working together as a team. This central organization can be either formal or informal. Examples of formal organizations are holding company boards, protector committees, and/or family councils An example of an informal organization is a group of actively engaged family members or owners communicating regularly and making decisions together. This central entity oversees and coordinates all the petal entities of the family enterprise. Family unity is imperative. Without it, the enterprise will struggle.

In Stage One, success was measured by gaining and keeping the control necessary to build and grow wealth in the flagship business. In Stage Two, success in the family enterprise is now measured by growth of the overall family wealth. This is measured by the output of all the wealth engines collectively, ranging from cash-generating businesses to risky new ventures and cash-sucking growth companies. Stage Two success is no longer measured by the performance of any particular business.

In the family enterprise stage, people now recognize the importance of non-financial family resources and begin to use them more effectively in service of growing overall family wealth. To keep evolving now requires an even broader range of family talent, plus leadership to manage the more diverse and resource-rich enterprise.

The Family Enterprise Model can be used by families to focus on building core unity among the actively engaged family members. If you keep working on the skills you developed in Stage One, a unified family can enforce critical behaviors that increase your chances of survival. The most important ones are (1) lifelong learning and development, (2) timely decision making, (3) support of family leaders, and (4) buy-in around critical initiatives.

Success in Stage Two improves your chances of survival because you focus more resources on developing wider strategies, creating more wealth engines, and executing these plans. The real growth opportunity for families in this stage involves developing and improving your internal responsiveness—how fast and well you can respond to the needs of the entities in your system. When one petal entity needs resources, you can coordinate among all the other petals to deliver them. Good timing, together with selecting the right resources, will help them build momentum, speed you toward success, or both.

For example, take Mulliez. This leading French family enterprise is focused on retailing, best known for the hypermarket Auchan, and now in the fourth generation of family leadership. Mulliez family members have launched more than twenty retailing companies, some bigger than others, all supported by funding from the family enterprise that aims to encourage starting up compelling new businesses.[7]

Both the Three-Circle Model and the Family Enterprise Model focus on the enterprising family as an organization. In the family business stage, the organization is formal and well defined: it is the flagship business. In the family enterprise stage, the organization can be formal or informal. It can even be a family governance body with voluntary membership.

In spite of having evolved from an earlier stage, family enterprise is still inward looking. It tends to focus on the development of the core group of engaged family members who will assume well-defined roles within the organization. It does not naturally center-prise (that is, focus on talent development of the broader family as a core shared activity). So, family enterprise tends not to deliver high performance as a broad resource developer. It is not optimal for engaging human capital both inside and outside the family.

This organization-focused approach of family enterprise *develops talent to serve the organization*. Compare that to the greater potential power you can get from a people-focused approach, where the organization facilitates investments in people to thrive.

As a family business advisor, I often have to guide families through the challenge of engaging less-involved family members. These are family members who have not found a place for themselves within the family enterprise. So often, this problem occurs because the family enterprise puts too much emphasis on asking less-involved family members questions, like "What can you (individual family members) do for the family enterprise?" Instead, why not answer their questions, like "How could the family enterprise support me as an individual?" The organizational culture of the family enterprise often feels unwelcoming to family members with no official roles. As a result, their already weak links to it become even weaker over time. Typically, the family enterprise never benefits from the resources they already possess—or will acquire in the future.

At the same time, family members usually maintain close relationships with each other. That is just what families do naturally. In plain language, people like to socialize with each other and maybe collaborate on work-related projects as they occur organically. Families are bottom-up organic systems, not top-down organizations. Families are informal, not formal by nature. Family members enjoy shared identities even when their values, mission, and vision don't completely align with those of the core family leaders running the family enterprise.

Don't be surprised, even if your family becomes spread out all over the globe, if your kitchens smell the same. That's what a member of my research team discovered when interviewing one well-known multigenerational business family with a dozen family branches or more.

The team was invited to conduct research at several locations, including the private residences of family members, in different countries. One day, commenting on the excellent hospitality, and adding that something seemed familiar, the team was asked, "Oh? Do you mean the soufflé?" Wafting in from the kitchen came the signature fragrance of a soufflé being cooked to the family recipe passed down generationally. The team had recently been served the same dessert in a different house in another country! Family members' tastes were so well known, that all over the world, this family's kitchens tend to smell the same. They cook the same food, use the same spices, love the same meals, and gather around similar hearths expecting other family members to drop by on short notice. It's a simple but powerful way they've organically reinforced the shared identities that individuals have treasured over generations.[8]

But for those whose interests differ greatly from those at the core of the family enterprise, they just don't enjoy attending formal family council meetings. It seems burdensome to decide on how to govern the family enterprise, especially when it has minimal relevance to their personal lives. Any family business advisor who has worked to improve a family enterprise over a decade or more has seen this natural change in interest—and it is often in the downward direction, meaning dwindling participation.

It's important to keep in mind that *the family is not an organization*. It's a collection of individuals with shared identities, unique talents, and the Four Capitals that they each possess. What are the Four Capitals? These are financial, intellectual, human, and social forms of capital. The best way to remember them is by using the mnemonic, FISH. (For more detail, see Chapter 2.)

All together, these Four Capitals are what make up the pool of potential resources that the family enterprise organization can harness in order to drive the wealth engines of today and tomorrow. Besides contributing talent, know-how, and social networks, family members can also contribute their financial capital, either by investing their independent wealth well, starting up successful businesses outside of the family enterprise, or inheriting significant wealth from the "in-law" parent (whether in the maternal or paternal line). Evolving well, the family enterprise broadens and taps into a richer pool of resources to further its own goals. Evolving badly, some family members de-link and float away. This can shrink the family enterprise's future opportunity set.

The drawbacks of the organization-centric approach to best practices in family enterprise went unnoticed before the New Digital Age. But now there's an open war for talent. By all accounts, non-family companies should win this war. To do that, non-family companies will have to reckon seriously with disruption and reputational issues. As the Edelman survey data shows, people have developed trust issues in many business, political, and social interactions today. Lack of confidence in products, services, governance, or processes can drive talent away. And innovators on the edge have proven time and again that they can win and become leaders of disrupted or emerging industries overnight. Given this context for non-family companies, family enterprises can step up to win. But they're in danger of being left behind if they stand still.

The Family Enterprise Model has room for improvement. But how?

Stage Three: The Family Ecosphere

The answer is: you've got to set your family enterprise in motion!

One of the major differences between families in Stage Three and those in other stages lies in their goal. In a family ecosphere, the goal is to try and develop each and every rising generation member into a Phoenix (i.e., an exceptional leader in their area of mastery), instead of choosing only a few among the litter to develop. Another difference lies in the structure. The family ecosphere is flexibly arrayed as a distributed system, linking a string of Phoenixes and their innovations to the family enterprise core of highly engaged family leaders. This is an interactive environment where the world can link in. It's free and open like any ecosphere, with interdependent parts that are both natural and man-made, in which the family enterprise and all its stakeholders must thrive so that its power source can be protected and replenished.

Imagining your own Family Ecosphere Model can spark a highly creative, entrepreneurial, and Future-Forward innovation culture. That is because innovation often happens organically on the edge of your industry or sector, while transformation usually needs to occur at the core to amplify its impact. This way of designing the family enterprise broadens the pool of trusted talent. Talented family members can:

1. *Be deployed* to collect data "in the outer galaxies" and be exposed to new ideas;

2. *Gather resources* such as new ideas, non-family talent, investment opportunities, and collaborative projects;

3. *Carry out experiments*; and

4. Bring them back to *catalyze the core*, if experiments were successful on the edge.

The core family enterprise then selects, modifies, and incorporates the suitable ideas into its system. Thereafter, it broadcasts these new ideas to the other outposts and/or passes them down to the next generation.

This is how the family organization amplifies the impact of its diverse resources. A well-functioning family ecosphere is the business family's version of a distributed system, with a stable core and an active edge interacting flexibly so it can continuously replenish the resources available to the family enterprise.

Imagining a family ecosphere, then building one, is an activity that represents a profound shift in mindset on the part of family members. Their focus has changed forever. They are now focused on the future of family excellence. From now on, their mechanism for survival will be to maximize performance of all family members, then to harvest those performances for the benefit of the family enterprise—and for all.

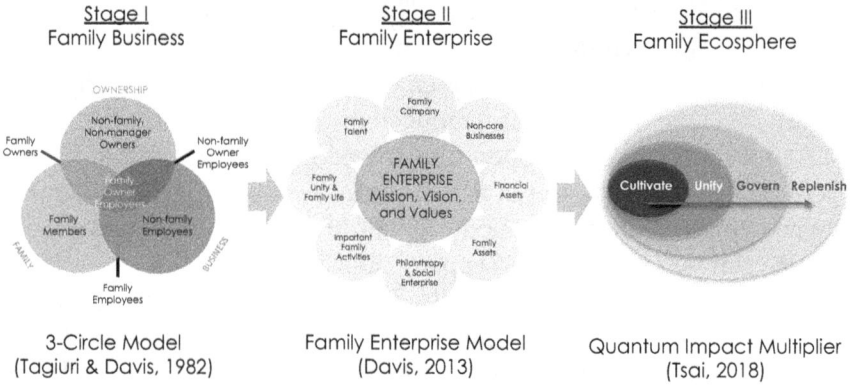

Stage I
Family Business

Stage II
Family Enterprise

Stage III
Family Ecosphere

3-Circle Model
(Tagiuri & Davis, 1982)

Family Enterprise Model
(Davis, 2013)

Quantum Impact Multiplier
(Tsai, 2018)

Three-Stage Evolution of the Family Business System. (Florence C. Tsai, 2018)

The major insights that led me to develop the Family Ecosphere Model have been drawn from a decade of client work with enterprising families all over the world. From East to West, it's always true, even in a highly unified family, that many family members' level of engagement with the family organizations may ebb and flow over time. But well-run family organizations do help family members switch on the Longevity DNA they share—their identities, values, and mission.

I came to realize that the mothership of family enterprise is not the family business. The mothership is not the family enterprise organization with the engaged family leadership group at the center, either. The mothership is in the family group, where the Longevity DNA is replenished and passed down from generation to generation. The mothership is the organic collection of shared identities established from birth and reinforced through family interactions that helps the business family survive and thrive into the next generation. And it is the collective talents and resources of the family that individuals use to help each other, as families naturally do and have done for millennia. The mothership itself is somewhat amorphous. But you can definitely feel its presence. When the mothership sets sail, she does so to give close support to family members, especially rising leaders. Think of the mothership as what sustained Tony Stark in his struggle for survival. Or what drove Heracles to complete his twelve labors, even when he suffered setbacks.

Let's take a closer look at what generally happens in families around the world. When family members venture out, they rely on the mothership for certain resources, like validation and perhaps social or intellectual capital, even if no financial resources are given. Family members tend to mostly sail across the same waters–whether it's a lake, a fjord, or an ocean. When they land, they mostly march in the same direction. But here's what they don't do. They don't march exactly to the same drum beat, and they hardly ever take the same tack. This, to me, is an important finding. I hope you'll agree. Family members do not, and usually won't, serve as implementers of pre-fab directives from the family organization. They want to individually feel inspired to march in the same direction as the family group, where the family organization serves as the beacon. They want to play a part in charting out the general direction, which is most effective when partly planned (top-down) and partly organic (bottom-up). And this general group direction also has to fit well with their individual passions and ambitions.

The mothership is the renewable power supply that feeds the family enterprise organization. And if the core family leaders use the organization well, they can turn it into a Quantum Machine that builds a force multiplier for the benefit of the organization and its stakeholders—doing good while doing good business.

Rising leaders with East Asian origins have a great metaphor that can help you visualize the power and enduring advantage that is rarely unleashed by family enterprise. In auto racing (even more true in motorcycle racing), they say, "弯道超车," or "you've got to pass in the corners." This takes masterful control of a high-performance machine coming into the corner, where you are jostling for position in a crowd, and then explosive power coming out. If control is lacking, the vehicle flips. Game over.

A combustion engine uses non-renewable resources, so I like to think of the family enterprise engine as a turbine. A turbine uses renewable energy, like water, that is constantly replenished in the family. Imagine your evolving family enterprise as the turbine that drives a Quantum Machine. There are gears driving all your activities from the core to the periphery. They harness the potential of all the collective resources of the entire business family. Imagine those renewable family resources as the mill pond in E.I. DuPont's black powder factory.

With a family ecosphere model, you can make use of a wider, trusted family network that can bring new innovations from the edge back to the core. (How to do this is detailed in Chapter 2.) With more people out on the edge, you're outward-looking and better positioned in the world to scout and recruit non-family talent that shares similar cultural DNA. When those people collaborate with the family enterprise, you create a resource force field to build new wealth engines based on diverse human talent.

In Stage Three evolution, the main job for the seasoned family leader is to transform the resources of the mothership into a force multiplier. The main growth area for you and everyone to focus on is adopting a shared, Future-Forward mindset in the family as part of your Longevity DNA. You need to learn and practice staying collectively focused on selecting, solving, and profiting from emerging problems whose time horizons are too far out for the short-term-minded CEOs of public companies to act on. For maximum advantage, your horizons should even be beyond the range of professional asset managers.

The Family Ecosphere. (Florence C. Tsai, 2018)

The Family Ecosphere Model lets you see how to combine all the unique competitive advantages of the enterprising family—long-term thinking in a renewable pool of resources plus an expanding pool of loyal, talented stakeholders—and turn them into wealth creation engines that generate uncommon profits and beneficial social impact. This is the moment when family enterprise takes a quantum leap and evolves from an inward-looking organization into an outward-looking family ecosphere with ever expanding influence, access to resource pools, and the ability to create impact multipliers from these resources.

The Quantum Machine Defined

Think of the Quantum Machine as the gear system in your high-performance race car. The beauty of a great, low-friction gear system is that it amplifies the power source by delivering more torque or speed.

Everybody knows what acceleration is, but you may have forgotten what torque is. Torque is the force required to do the heavy-lifting when you're on the move: either to get a ship or a locomotive underway from a standstill, or pass a slow-moving truck on a mountain road, or drive a heavy vehicle out of the corner on the racetrack, or boost a rocket. When Han Solo tells Chewbacca to "punch it!" in "Star Wars," the ship has to deliver huge torque for hyperdrive. When you slow down for a big pothole in the road, your car has to deliver torque to get that wheel up and out of the hole. It's the same in family enterprise. The Quantum Machine can deliver torque or acceleration, whichever one you need, when you need it.

Have you ever driven a hybrid vehicle? When you hit the brakes, your car uses that heat to charge the battery. As you drive, power is being both expended and gathered by the same vehicle. It's the same with the Quantum Machine. You design it as a two-way gear system that transmits power and speed to the distributed parts of your family system at the levels you require, and later delivers resources and information back to the core. Wherever two gears meet (for example, where the family business connects with a new joint venture partner), there should be a family leader acting as a lever, controlling the direction of energy flow.

Depending on the gear system you design, you transmit your power differently for the needs of each gear in the machine.

Thinking about your family enterprise petals as gears in a machine can help you understand the range of strength, speed, and momentum you can get for the same power (resource) output.

Centerprise—Build and Fire Up That Machine!

If you have a family enterprise in place, or if your non-family company looks like a family enterprise, you already have some existing petals around the flower. Maybe you've got some operating businesses with one or more companies in them. Maybe you've got a family office for making investments. Maybe your altruism has created one or more philanthropic organizations, an institution, or even a social enterprise that operates for profit or shares its profits. All these were designed and built by the family leaders. The organizations themselves are ultimately controlled by their owners. This is the group that controls the resources, like the board of directors in a non-family company. And in family enterprise, when people refer to "the owners," they usually mean the generation of seasoned family leaders, even though the ownership group is usually larger. Those seasoned family leaders get a lot of respect. They are usually regarded as highly as the elders in most families.

Now's the time, seasoned leaders reading this book, to inspire all your other family members to imagine their part in the evolution of your family ecosphere. It's your job to lead and collaboratively figure out how to gear them into the Quantum Machine that you'll power (with resources you control) from the family enterprise organization. In accomplishing this, the family enterprise provides the beacon, the materials, and the tool kit, while each family member builds their own sailing ship—airplane, seagoing vessel, land vehicle, or bicycle—and decides if they want to follow the beacon.

The Quantum Machine offers a gearing approach to rapid change, with adaptable tools that help you stay agile. At the center, transformation is now possible because more family members want to engage. The desire to contribute to the enterprising family is already in their DNA. This gene is now being expressed more broadly, because you've encouraged individual adoption of desirable traits through the creation of new gears—gears of their own

design—that are supported by the collective family resources. This
is empowering.

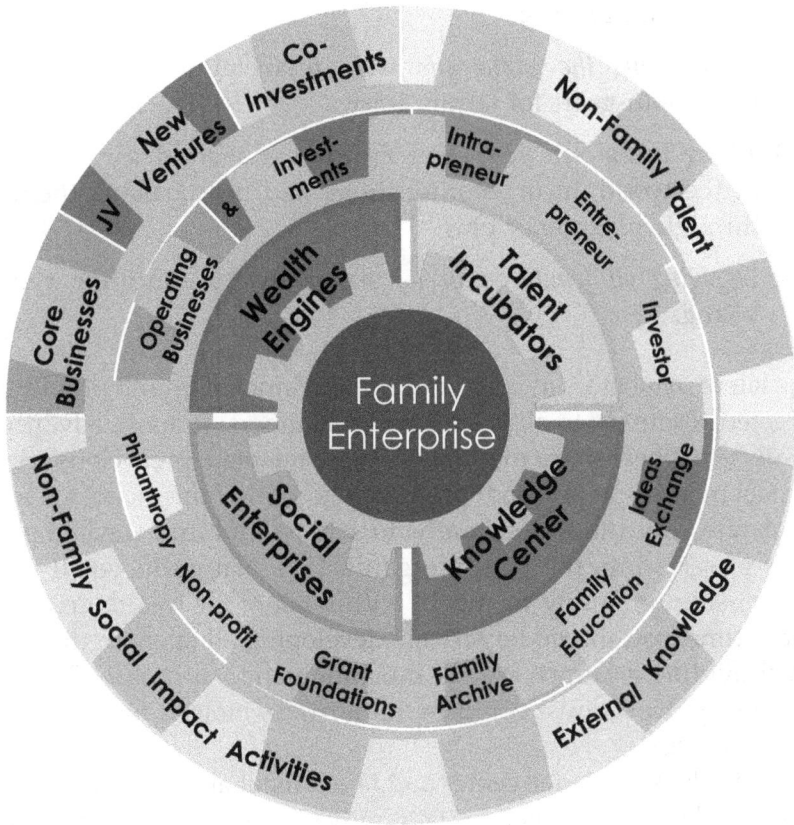

The Quantum Machine. (Florence C. Tsai, 2018)

At the heart of building a Quantum Machine is the work that
the family organization leaders do to centerprise. This means to
make investments for people to thrive, from the innermost core of
the family ecosphere to the farthest outpost. This involves building
out and firing up the core gears: a knowledge center and a talent
incubator.

The knowledge center focuses on enriching the organizational
wisdom, human capital, and intellectual capital you possess in
order to cultivate all family members—plus, some non-family folks
who share similar outlooks and have the potential to be long-term
collaborators.

Your core should now focus on:

1. *Transmitting* family values, vision, and mission out into your gear organizations;

2. *Replenishing the mothership* with financial resources and using your gears for family spirit;

3. *Taking in the new ideas* that family members discover out in the world, incorporating them, and broadcasting them through other gears; plus

4. *Engaging all family members,* especially by educating the young.

The talent incubators focus on developing innovators and providing targeted resources to all adult family members. In more advanced family ecospheres, you might also invite talented, precocious teens to start incubating personal projects. The goal of the incubator is to accelerate your innovators' paths to success and find ways to gear their projects into the family organization. Naturally, you'll start by focusing on family members with a talent for wealth creation, but in time, you should be actively developing all talent in the family. Providing a launch pad is the enlightened approach. Today's college-age biochemist could be tomorrow's biotech founder. You never know.

With the knowledge center and talent incubators running effectively, and with replenishing the family's financial resources as Job No. 1, next is for the seasoned family leader(s) to take on the role of Chief Capital Allocation Officer. In this role, the leader is entrusted to move resources to the gears that need torque or acceleration or both. The primary responsibility is to control the one-way flow of resources from the family to the family organization. The secondary responsibilities are securing adequate resources for family members as needed while they are building their individual gears; then helping gear-in new projects, satellite activities, or wealth engines into the family enterprise. This job requires experience and sound judgment.

For example, when you spot a young family member doing well in Silicon Valley, consider helping maintain that momentum. You could provide mentorship from any one of the appropriate family engines. Or offer an attractive employment opportunity in the family company. Or even make an investment in the Silicon Valley company itself. You could even license the new technology for use by the core.

This way, the family elders can guide the family organization to achieve quantum performance by creating a virtuous cycle. (See the figure below.) Innovation culture leads to a Future-Forward mindset, which motivates you to invest in all family members, then enables you to grow and harvest all Four Capitals.

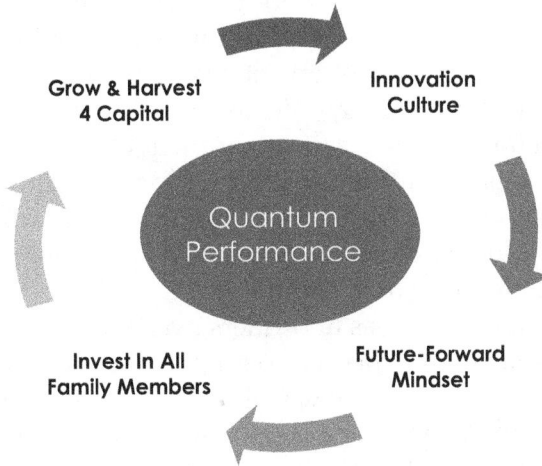

Cycle of Quantum Performance. (Florence C. Tsai, 2018)

The Five Arrows of the Rothschild Family

A few well-known family ecospheres have been in operation for a very long time, with family talent pools that have produced several generations of leaders and several Phoenixes, plus a global, distributed system of organizations that were successful long before the dawn of the digital age. One of these is the Rothschild family ecosphere.

It's a long story, so here are the highlights. Quiz at eleven! Just kidding.

The founder, Mayer Amschel Rothschild (1744–1812), set high expectations for his five sons, all of whom followed him into business. Rothschild invented modern banking. Forbes calls him the seventh most influential businessman of all time, credited with introducing "concepts such as diversification, rapid communication, confidentiality, and high volume."[9] So yeah, he had a Future-Forward mindset.

Based in Frankfurt, Rothschild's coin trading business attracted royal clients during a period of political instability on the continent of Europe. His clients trusted him, so whenever they needed to flee to safety, Rothschild became their property manager. He could leverage their vast resources in clever ways to boost his own. Historian Niall Ferguson details how in his two-volume study, *The House of Rothschild*, which I highly recommend.[10] The Rothschild family history below has been drawn from those books.

In 1798, the five Rothschild brothers—Amschel, Solomon, Nathan, Kalmann, and James—went into partnership with their father and set up banking operations in five cities—Frankfurt (before there was a Germany), Vienna, London, Naples, and Paris. They chose a quiver of five arrows for their logo, still in use today. Their father was an authoritarian who transmitted a set of family values that was imprinted deeply in the family, but there was no central, top-down business. It was highly entrepreneurial. The only way the brothers could communicate, work together, or transfer resources was by horses and riders overland, or else by sea. So they built the fastest and best courier system in the world, innovating outside their core industry. It still wasn't fast enough to manage their growth. The stressors of a war-torn age fated them all to become Phoenixes, each brother crashing and burning his business at least once, then rising from the ashes to rebuild stronger.

Over generations, as the family pool kept growing, ownership of the Rothschild family resources spread out into many family branches. The family organization expanded, making major contributions in a mind-boggling array of industries. Operations involved hundreds of organizations, from industrial business conglomerates on every continent and philanthropy on an international scale, to generations of British politicians, groundbreaking scientific institutions, and world-famous winemaking.

The stable pool of resources continued to provide rising leaders with proving-grounds and successful ventures. When the First World War broke out in 1914, hostilities separated family members based on their citizenship. Business and ownership ties were permanently severed between the branches. During the Second World War, things got even worse when Axis powers confiscated the Jewish family's resources, hunted the Rothschilds down, and even murdered family members. The cracks in the family pool contributed to widening wealth inequality between surviving branches.

But throughout all this, the family has remained united and highly entrepreneurial for eight generations, producing global leaders in many fields. Individual family members still regularly participate together in social enterprise. Family branches work to safeguard the family's Longevity DNA in London at The Rothschild Archive, a research institution.

Replenishing the family pool had become part of the family's goals by the late 20th century. After a decade working toward reunification, the banking businesses of two family branches in the U.K. and France merged their financial resources in 2007.[11] In 2012, Jacob, Lord Rothschild, founder of publicly-traded Rothschild Investment Trust (RIT), an investment vehicle in which all family members can participate, worked with David Rockefeller to form a strategic partnership with Rockefeller Financial Services.[12] This further replenished the pool of resources in America, where members of many family branches have lived since the Second World War.[13] RIT sold its stake five years later in 2017.[14] One hundred years after World War I, the Rothschild family pool has now been rebuilt to contain all family branches. The family ecosphere is still thriving, with at least three family wineries and several distinct banking operations.

The Evolution of Governance

Governance of your family organization remains critical in a family ecosphere system. Governance, for business families, is there to protect the interests of at least three groups that are sometimes in conflict: the owners, the business employees, and the family. Whether you're a founder-led family business with informal governance, or a multigeneration family enterprise with a family constitution, an assembly, and a policy handbook, your enduring advantage depends on family unity. The family won't stay together long if safeguards or checks and balances aren't in place.

Your core work is still done in the family organization setting—housed under a governance structure. This is where family members who are interested will contribute to building explicitly shared values, vision, and a Future-Forward mission for building resources and value with the Quantum Machine. Then they will convert that value to financial capital as needed, for use by the enterprise or by the family.

As you evolve, keep the governance structures you have. Only let them go, thoughtfully and intentionally, when they no longer serve the interests of family members. Never jettison good governance to further the interests of any single petal entity. Keep your focus, in the digital age, on achieving agile governance structures to address change as new, challenging issues need to be examined and new actors gear into the system in your family's ever-expanding ecosphere. Remember that a hallmark of good governance is strategic timeliness. This is the art of mastering how to make sure you're having the right conversations at the right times among the right people, striking a balance between fairness and decisiveness.

Globally, we see that governance also is moving from centralized control through rules and processes to distributed self-governance, where the focus is on cultivating meetings of the mind among the people who need to be "in the room."

Concentric Circles of Influence

In Asian philosophy, Neo-Confucians believe that in order to achieve universal harmony, one starts with cultivating oneself, then puts one's house in order, then governs the community through mutual understanding of cultural norms. Only then will harmony be naturally accomplished. It can be adapted for family ecospheres like this:

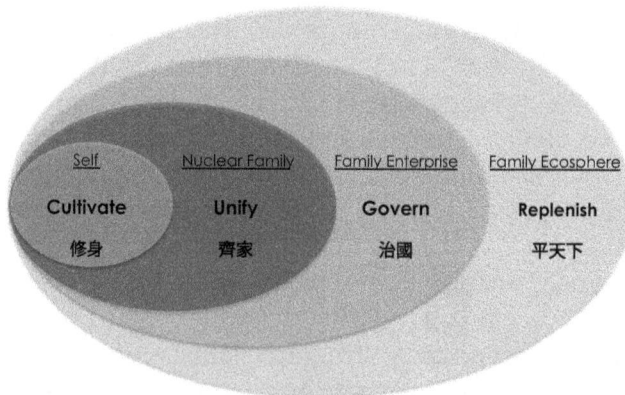

Self	Nuclear Family	Family Enterprise	Family Ecosphere
Cultivate	Unify	Govern	Replenish
修身	齊家	治國	平天下

Family Ecosphere Quantum Impact Multiplier. (Florence C. Tsai, 2018)

This voluntary system of shared ownership (instead of one that handcuffs family members together by the family trust) is more outward-looking and will motivate family members on the edges not to drift further away from the family organization, but to move closer. This is what you want: more of the external change agents and disrupters remaining part of the family. This strategy has already been proven successful in non-family companies. Chinese internet behemoths Alibaba and Tencent, acting much like mother-ships in a family ecosphere, have both built influential ecosystems that support former engineers exiting the company to create their own start-ups. The new ventures are often backed by the mother-ship—and sometimes even acquired by it at a later date. About 50% of the market value of publicly listed Tencent consists of invest-ments in its ecosystem companies.[15]

Conclusion

Thinking Future-Forward, with quantum results on your mind, is a new way to look at your family enterprise and how it can win in the digital age. You already have the Longevity DNA stored securely in the family pool, where you can spot, develop, and deploy rising leaders, then deliver focused power to the opportunities they offer. That DNA is waiting to be activated by the wise senior leader who's ready, like E.I. Du Pont, to design a family ecosphere and build it with ironclad but nimble components to transform an unknown future.

CHAPTER **2**

Longevity DNA

$$Longevity = \sum_{0}^{\infty} (capacity\ for\ transformation)$$
To survive, innovate at the edge and adapt at the core.

Leadership and Innovation Culture at Corning

Before the 1970s, there were no venture capitalists. Even harder to believe, you couldn't stream cable. This is a story about how Longevity DNA gave us high speed internet.

Tech research today is more distributed among universities and VCs, but for most of the 20th century it happened deep inside big companies, where you had to be recruited as an employee to actually invent stuff. One of the first industrial research labs started up in 1908 at a second-generation family company in upstate New York. Today, that company is publicly-traded, and it reported revenue of $10 billion for 2017. Ten percent of that will go back into R&D. That's how it has always been done at Corning, the Houghton family business founded in 1851.[1] And that's how, for 168 years, the Houghton family has imprinted the organization with their Longevity DNA.

The family's ownership has dwindled below 3%, which isn't enough to control Corning any more, but Houghtons led the company or chaired the board for five generations until 2007. That's a lot of financial capital spent making long-term bets. What did they get for it?

To find out, let's go back to 1956. That's when legendary Houghton family member Katharine Hepburn earns her second Oscar nomination for "The Rainmaker," also starring Burt Lancaster. 1956 is also the year the term "fiber optics" is coined, referring to a whole category of products that use optical glass drawn in thin strands to transmit electrical impulses and light. Corning is an industrial supplier in the glass business. So Corning scientists start exploring fiber optics for certain technical uses. Engineers develop products but sales are modest—less than 1% of total revenue.

45

Ten years later, it's a different use of fiber optics (as optical wave-guides) that draws the interest of Corning scientists. The British government wants to explore potential replacements for copper wire in building out a new communications infrastructure—something that can carry more traffic. But the technology is at very early stages of development. Pursuing fiber optics for telecom at Corning can only be described as highly speculative. But since the most talented scientists in the lab want to go for it, and since fiber optics research uniquely suits Corning's expertise, management green-lights the program.

Almost a decade of fully funded research goes by without a product ready for commercialization. Meanwhile, the company is struggling financially. By the early 1970s, senior managers consider scrubbing the optic fiber program. Chuck Lucy, the business development manager, asks his boss for a commitment to continue research if he can get outside funding.

Chuck embarks on an odyssey but comes back from Europe and Japan with no deals. The old-economy partners he contacted are big, vertically integrated behemoths, some even operating their own copper mines. Corning's new tech will bring huge disruption. After much effort, Chuck is finally able to secure J/V funding for 50/50 co-development with Siemens in 1973.

Now Corning's investment has to keep pace with its partner. The costs start to go up. In 1975, for the second time in five years, the team at Corning has to decide whether to push ahead on optic fiber with the Siemens J/V, scale it back dramatically, or even exit. Siemens is a highly respected partner. It's a matter for the Chairman to decide.

From the perspective of the research team, based on results, the project is on the brink of failure. Will the family leader take the same view? If you were Amo Houghton, Chairman of Corning, how would you make this decision?

Amo Houghton decides to ask Dr. James B. Fisk for his opinion. Dr. Fisk sits on the Corning board and also happens to be Chairman of Bell Telephone Laboratories, a subsidiary of AT&T since 1925. Dr. Fisk says that fiber optics will be very big. He advises to keep it going.

In retrospect, it seems easy to see how this remark might have switched on the Houghton Longevity DNA, creating important momentum. As you might expect from a cousin of Katharine Hepburn, Amo Houghton isn't one to give up. He responds to the crisis, not just by committing funds, but also by bringing in Boston Consulting Group to study the world telecom market.

BCG concludes that if Corning is to win, they have to achieve three objectives:

1. Develop and protect Corning's technical leadership position, including vigorous defense of patents.

2. Find a way to sell optical fiber to AT&T.

3. Move quickly to expand Corning's positioning in international markets.

Amo Houghton approves a substantial financial investment, and the R&D team enters what Chuck Lucy terms "the money sucking phase." A crackerjack team is hired, consisting of engineers and creative, savvy production people who are great problem solvers—and most important, people who can work together to make it happen. Finally, the perfect leader for this team, David Duke, is brought in from another division.

Yesterday at Corning, David Duke was on a fast track with line responsibility for one thousand employees and $100 million in revenue. Today he's being moved to a project with six employees and less than $1 million in revenue, with orders to build manufacturing capability and scale a business that doesn't exist. They need to drive production costs down to, or below, the cost of the copper wires that currently transmit all telecommunications. It's understandable if he quits. Instead, something lights a fire in David Duke.

David Duke gets how high the stakes are. Going against the grain of the hierarchical R&D culture, he challenges the conclusion of the BGC study, arguing that it doesn't go far enough. To succeed in such a competitive environment, Corning has to move even more quickly and aggressively. David Duke thinks it's unacceptable to keep pace with competitors like Bell Labs. "When your competition is much bigger, matching it isn't good enough. If we tie, we lose."

By 1982, Corning is producing optical fiber with revenues of $10 million on a $100 million investment. Was it money down the drain? If not, where is all that financial value stored?

Corning has converted its financial investment into a different form of capital: intellectual property (IP), also known as intellectual capital. $100 million is now locked inside twelve key patents in fiber optics technology—a strategy the team copied from its arch rival,

Bell Labs, notorious for ring fencing its innovations. But does this intellectual capital have any value at all?

Then, in January 1982, something happens out of Corning's control that seals the fate of the fiber optics program forever. The U.S. Department of Justice breaks up AT&T as part of an anti-trust settlement. Suddenly, Corning's market opens up. With more customers, it has leverage to compete with AT&T. Following BCG's game plan, Corning wins an early patent infringement lawsuit that blocks competition and protects its markets. Corning will come to dominate the sector. The company and the family will harvest their investment financially, with handsome gains.

Amo Houghton's Longevity DNA

All this was possible because of the effects of Longevity DNA. Corning's family owners had already established a long-term vision, with proof in their annual reinvestment in R&D projects that exceeded five or even ten years. (Outside the company, the Houghtons also made consistent stakeholder investments in community development that continue today.) By 1965, the Houghton family had successfully passed its Longevity DNA down to the fifth-generation business leader.

When Amo Houghton was tested as a leader and made his choice to double down on fiber optics research and empower new, "inside outsider" management,[2] it gave David Duke the confidence to risk his own career progression in support of a new phase in the innovation—the practical phase of bringing products to market. When that happened, Duke's choice to accept his risky assignment was compelling, so his leadership was accepted, even though he had no prior experience in the department. By David Duke's comments, made when he was looking back on success, we sense that his excitement was contagious, and his sense of urgency built momentum.

Finally, all this was possible because of luck. Nobody can time the breakup of a monopoly or predict the outcome of a patent dispute, as you know well if you've been following the twists and turns in the fight between Samsung and Apple. Good fortune can strike at any time, but it takes patience to increase the odds of good luck happening to you.

And because all this was possible at Corning, fiber optic cable now carries 65,000 times more information than copper. We wouldn't have high speed internet without it.

The Edge and the Core

It's worth repeating that the secret to longevity is the ability to transform, because change is inevitable, while transformation needs to be an intentional effort. More innovation is now happening on the edge of organizations, rather than at the core. You need to pay attention to it.

With the family organization, you have the built-in advantage of your Longevity DNA to act on opportunities others can't afford. Your core probably has a light footprint—perhaps in the family office, in the family holding company, on the protector committee of the family trust, or in some other command center—and can be as mobile as your next family retreat. Plus, you already have an array of different organizations, like operating companies you control or the family office, that you can engage for innovation. So, as discussed in the previous chapter, you can link the edge and the core with gears of your own design. You can add gears as needed for leverage. Then, through family investment, you can control the speed and torque required for each innovation to bear fruit, given the resources you provide.

This chapter focuses on what those family investments can be, and how to use them in designing the gearing system of your Quantum Machine.

British Theater's Quantum Machine

Let's look at how it works in the entertainment industry. Consider a sector of live performances: British theater, a very good example of a Quantum Machine.

The core of the industry is in The West End—Central London's largest commercial district, comparable to Midtown Manhattan or the 8ème Arrondissement in Paris. Successful West End productions may run for decades. Agatha Christie's "The Mousetrap," the longest-running production in the world, has played in The West End since 1952.[3]

Every summer, new material gets tested by Britain's mainstream professional talent—literally on the Fringe. That's the Edinburgh Festival Fringe, in Scotland, the world's largest arts festival, with its own chairman and board of directors.

In August 2017, there were more than 53,000 Fringe performances of 3,300 shows by established artists and entrepreneurial talent alike.[4] All shows are open-access; there are no juries, no gatekeepers. If you can find a venue and afford to mount a production, the stage is yours. You can "gear in" as you like, deciding what types of resources to invest—and how much—to get the results you want to measure. So, the environment is wide open for innovation.

The Guardian describes the Edinburgh Fringe as an ecosphere, where cheap feeder venues attract first-time producers and, over the course of several seasons, deliver them up to stages equipped to mount shows with progressively high production values. Venue costs run from free to uber-pricey, and ticket prices are unregulated, so the economics of the Fringe are as chaotic as the atmosphere that lured over two million ticket buyers in 2017.[5] The Fringe is also part of a shared economy and delivers big benefits to stakeholders. It contributed the lion's share of income to the city's net festival economy of GBP 143 million, with a multiplier effect of GBP 279 million in 2015.[6] These numbers also make the Fringe a viable incubator for innovations in other industries, like transportation; hospitality; tourism; and food and beverage.

Fringe theater, like all innovations, is risky business, but concentrating everyone's efforts spreads the risk.[7] Successful work attracts new resources and takes you back to London, where new productions are mounted Off West End and make their way to the West End. That's where famous screen actors often appear in starring roles to boost the box office.

Average production costs in London are small, compared to what it costs to bring shows to Broadway. Eventually, the most successful West End productions, like "Stomp,"[8] do end up on Broadway, doubling their market. So, pushing innovative material out from the West End is good business. 2017 was a record-breaking year for London's West End,[9] with 15 million tickets sold and box office receipts of GBP700 million (about $1 billion).[10] On Broadway, 13.5 million ticket sales generated $1.6 billion in revenue.[11]

As you can see, the Edinburgh Fringe creates an impact multiplier for successful innovators who can "gear in."

Now let's imagine that you have a rising leader in your family with potential for breakout success in the theater. She wants to test an innovation, and she's ready to mount a live performance or production. She remains open about the details. Here's what you can do with this opportunity to develop your family's Longevity DNA, with potentially quantum benefits for all.

First, you can mobilize the family in support of that entrepreneur and begin to gather professional knowledge and information that may be beyond her scope of expertise about the "known universe." You want to gain an understanding of all the types of resources required for success—including but not limited to financial resources (see below for a detailed discussion about this). Consider direct financial investment, partnerships, or co-investors; how much investment is likely to be required; when it will be needed; and what the investment horizon is likely to look like.

Your family organization can provide timely, focused knowledge and information to your entrepreneur about the quantum opportunity at the Fringe. Don't assume that the innovator has thought of every way to maximize value or impact. Listen closely and ask good questions. Have that discussion at the family ecosphere level, so everybody in the knowledge and information gear can learn from the exercise.

If the rising leader commits to a plan on the Fringe that involves you, it's time to turn the building blocks of your family organization into gears to help them gain certain advantages. Go back to the centerprising process to guide you through this strategic exercise, so you don't overlook key points of leverage with future benefits to the family ecosphere. For every resource you plan to offer, decide if you will "make or buy" the asset to be used by the innovator. Perhaps the family company has a U.K. subsidiary that could help form a production company. Or perhaps this is time to buy property for lease to the rising leader and their network. Scan your Quantum Machine for gears that can be used, or build a new one.

With those gears built to the right specifications, you can calibrate your Quantum Machine to link in effectively with the West End's, through the Fringe ecosystem. Then you can commit family resources strategically, anticipating future runs in London and New York, controlling the speed or torque as events progress. During the ups and downs of the odyssey to come, your unwavering commitment raises performance expectations that will develop your rising leader as a professional.

Permit me to congratulate you on your future success! All you'll have to do then is to convince your innovator to bring the fruits of that success back to the mothership. That's the final step in furthering the Longevity DNA you need.

To start getting this done, you need to set your family enterprise in motion as soon as possible. Do this by adopting and cultivating a new mindset.

Future-Forward Thinkers and Experimenters

You've heard of fashion forward style? It's a knack for wearing things that seem slightly edgy or offbeat today, but will become fashionable tomorrow. There's also Future-Forward style. This is the knack for being ahead of the curve. Future-Forward types can seem edgy, but they're good at perceiving unforeseen consequences. You recognize Future-Forward style in people who are curious, who are always learning and experimenting, who cultivate a perpetual state of becoming.

What does it mean to be Future-Forward? It's mostly a state of mind, where imagination, knowledge, decisiveness, and experience converge. You can see a sequence of future events unfold before your eyes. You have a sense of inhabiting the future. Advanced chess players, motorcyclists, climbers, and high-performance athletes know what this is. Some will have greater gifts, and some will develop their gifts more than others, but the evolving family, as a whole, needs to be hungry for this mindset.

After developing the Future-Forward state of mind, you need to add the skills of a practical realist. Learn to scan your environment, through your special Longevity DNA telescope, for information and data that don't just point to a business opportunity, they also fix that opportunity in space and time. Think of this as scouting for land in the open ocean. Then get a sense of how big the land mass is. This is quantifying your opportunity. Finally, if you want to influence future outcomes, build your appetite for commitment. Follow the most direct course to landfall. And remember, a tenant has little say in a homeowner's association meeting, so buy in.

The outlook and habits of Future-Forward people in family enterprise are those of practical futurists. They study mega trends and quantum shifts that upend large, broad distributions of capital that is already invested. Amo Houghton and his family at Corning were practical futurists when they envisioned the future for fiber optics to replace copper wire.

By this definition, entrepreneur Elon Musk would not be labeled a practical futurist for his commitment to SpaceX, the company he founded in 2002 to revolutionize space technology. Apart from developing the transportation sector for colonization (such as rocketry and spacecraft), there hasn't yet been a wide distribution of capital deployed for SpaceX's mission of "making life multiplanetary."[12] There are no present values for investments in resources for supporting life on Mars, for instance, so future values cannot be known, only guessed. Elon Musk is a Future-Forward pioneer in this regard, but not a practical futurist.

Practical futurists, by contrast, eliminate the guessing, as much as possible, to seize opportunities others can't afford.

Sinkhole Becomes Museum Piece: The Practical Futurist

Here's a recent example of how Chubb, a Future-Forward organization, tried to attract practical futurists through useful forecasting. In October 2018, The United Nations published a report that moved up the date, to 2040, of its forecast for devastating effects of rising sea levels that will affect coastal cities in the U.S., such as Miami. When *Business Insider* reported the story online, Chubb ran an ad with a provocative headline: "Sinkhole Becomes Museum Piece."[13] When I read that, I instantly imagined a ten million dollar estate, filled with priceless artwork, suddenly at the bottom of a sinkhole.

As a practical futurist, Chubb's witty ad might capture your attention and lead you to a new opportunity down a path that looks something like this.

You might do some Googling and learn that other news outlets have reported on a peer-reviewed study by Harvard professor Jesse Keenan, with Thomas Hill and Anurag Gumber, published in April 2018. It presented the first empirical evidence for climate change affecting real estate values in Miami Dade County, Florida.[14] The study's focus is primarily on the effects of elevation. Considering the United Nations report, this might raise deeper questions, leading you to make pretty specific forecasts about Miami real estate values in 2040, based on the availability of fresh water for all properties, not just those at lower elevations. Will there be enough fresh water? If not, where will fresh water come from? What needs to change for property owners to adapt and/or make use of brackish water for daily use, such as laundering, if no fresh water is available?

Now you see a quantifiable future problem: high likelihood of a systemic fresh water crisis in Miami. You see a market: all property owners with outdoor irrigation systems, washing machines, and other sensitive water-cooled machinery, such as centralized HVAC. And now there's a drop-dead date, 2040. For most investors, this information is meaningless. The 22-year time horizon is too long. But not in family enterprise, as we have seen in the Corning case. As a practical futurist equipped with Longevity DNA, your curiosity—triggered by an amusing insurance ad—may have led you to the brink of a viable business opportunity that others can't see or won't commit to.

When you can recognize practical futurism as a widely shared trait, the family should begin generally to encourage and support family members on the edge of the family organization who are Future-Forward thinkers and experimenters.

Here's how to do that.

At the core of your family organization is the gear for driving knowledge and information. Use that gear to constantly collect data about the future. Set up a system for processing it. Develop habits that ingrain a culture encouraging Future-Forward discussions. Set the technical level to attract the greatest number of participants. Start forming your views about the future. For major industries, families should discuss what they think will happen in 10-plus years.

Think about what happens to markets, society, natural resources, and so forth, given the implications of the data you trust. Determine what time horizon will lead to changes that will upend current industries where you have interest or know-how. Be sensitive to timing, but don't rush to any decisions if you don't need to. The research process can take many years, and you may decide to launch a few small ships in different directions with a bit of capital first, and then increase that capital amount when the family sees that milestones are reached.

Corning does this regularly. They're always looking for what to develop in Area X (meaning new technologies and emerging market opportunities). When former Chairman Jamie Houghton was a rising leader, just named Chief Strategy Officer, he conducted a portfolio review. His own strategy didn't differ from the one he had inherited:

> The company would transfer resources from the industries of the past (lightbulb glass and refractories) to the industries of the future (optical waveguides and industrial biotechnology), while maintaining "self-sustaining" and "cash-generating" industries of the present (consumer products, TV glass, automotive products, and ophthalmic glass).[15]

Once you decide on a Future-Forward route, go to the family pool of resources for greenlight. Choose a captain for this voyage, set aside resources for launch, and pass some or all of them to the family organization. Before you embark, instruct the family organization to gear the Quantum Machine so you can make or buy the vehicle/s you need (whether tapping into family or non-family talent) and link in with gears in other ecosystems if needed (such as identifying co-investors to share the risks). Make sure you have enough resources to land the ship. Then set sail.

It is the family, not any organization, that decides which future problem you want to solve and what solution you see for solving it. Leave it to wealth managers, advisors, or the family company, and the family will never see the total array of possibilities. Why not? Because your horizon is longer than theirs. In making bets for the long term, the risk tolerance for any service provider is probably lower than that of the family. However time-consuming, disciplining your family to do its own Future-Forward thinking forces you to keep making investments in new macro-trends.

That said, when scanning for future problems to solve, you should probably give more weight to what rising leaders are interested in—and then carefully assess their judgment.

As practical realists, the long-term voyages you embark on need to be sustainable. They need to be compelling, to keep your interest over the long term—possibly beyond the lifetimes of today's senior leaders.

Before embarking on any epic voyage, it's important that you develop increasingly high confidence that the effort will succeed. Your children will inherit the choices you make. If you're uncomfortable with that, perhaps it's better to pick opportunities that you can harvest, financially, during your own lifetime.

Committing to harvest a future opportunity by offering unique solutions to a future problem takes courage and creativity. The practical futurist behind any of these ventures always has to convince family members and owners to lend their resources.

Let's take a look at what those resources actually are.

The Four Capitals

Just like pillars that support a strong building, there are four kinds of capital. Your family decides how to use its resources in each of the Four Capitals to maximize the chances of success of your future opportunity.

All capital is convertible. That means you can grow wealth as one kind of capital, convert it for storage into another kind of capital, and deploy it in another form if you need to.

You need to nurture and develop all Four Capitals so your family can increase your odds, of not only growing wealth through several generations, but also growing it at a rate that will keep up with the exponential growth of your family group.

Wealth is made up of these forms of capital—financial, human, intellectual, and social. This is the order in which I rank them for gearing power, but the best way to remember them is by using the mnemonic FISH. It's so easy, in fact, that you can teach it to small children and teenagers.

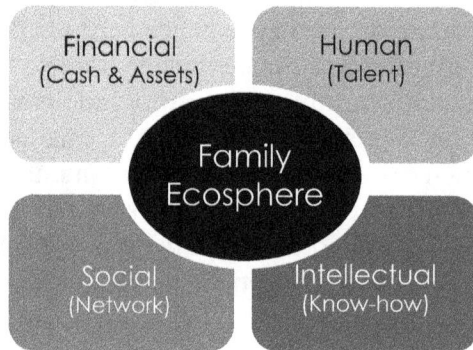

Four Capitals of the Family Ecosphere.

Financial capital includes money, real property, and all other kinds of negotiable instruments, like stocks, bonds, debt, foreign currencies, trusts, and other financial contracts. Most of the assets in this class are easily valued. Focusing on growing these assets is, essentially, all about making money.

You'll need financial capital for starting Future-Forward projects, because it takes a lot of torque to get them moving. The du Pont family financed their early American operations with a combination of cash (for which they exchanged equity, or shares in their company) and debt (which they promised to pay back with interest). At du Pont in the founding days at Eleutherian Mills, the family was painfully short of financial capital. So they made use of social capital instead.

Human capital produces the work that creates and builds your wealth. You've probably heard of "sweat equity." Sweat equity is human capital. To grow wealth for your family, you need to manage human capital, both inside the family and out.

Talent is the basis of all human capital. We value work by talent and scarcity. The level of your talent is measured along with how common it is to produce work that can be valued in any given context. Professional sports and Olympic competition give the best examples. Talented athletes in these elite circles win medals and get contracts. Contracts can be valued as financial capital.

At Eleutherian Mills, Irénée du Pont was the main source of human capital in the new family business for a long time. Later, Irénée's three sons all worked in the business. It's unclear what, if any, human capital Victor or Pierre du Pont provided to the gunpowder business, but as long as they lived, Irénée's brother and father continued building and converting social capital for the family ecosphere.

Take a look at people developing their talents. Do you notice that you tend to group them by their roles? This is natural. But there can be pitfalls when you focus too much on existing roles when developing or assessing talent. Since Thomas Jefferson has figured into the du Pont story, let's take him as an example of these pitfalls.

Jefferson is widely known for his role as a Founding Father of the United States, with a talent for philosophy and writing that got him the job of drafting the Declaration of Independence. He served two terms in the role of President, where his talent for politics was in high demand. Most of us also know that Jefferson was an accomplished architect, musician, farmer, and the inventor of the swivel chair who spoke and wrote five languages. Yet we tend to discount the value of those achievements. We shouldn't. Those talents served him well in lesser roles at various times by building social capital, preparing Jefferson for his political career, and advancing it from the Revolution to his Presidency. How many of us have sounded the deep talent base in our own extended family, let alone in the workplace? Make sure you keep spotting and developing talent (in yourself and others) even if it's not specific to any current role. It may become very valuable in a future role.

Non-family human capital also needs to be spotted and developed within the family ecosphere. You'll want to engage senior management, board members, scientists, and other contributors who can help you generate more financial assets.

Social capital includes your trusted relationships and human networks. You manage and develop these over time to generate more financial capital. And also for a more fulfilling life.

Irénée du Pont's gunpowder mill got off the ground with social capital. In fact, it's one of the most famous examples of the use of social capital in American history. Remember how his costs were skyrocketing out of control in 1803 to build a factory that had no orders? Here's how those orders got placed.

Thomas Jefferson was President of the United States at the time, and he had been quietly trying to solve a growing international problem for two years. Jefferson told Pierre du Pont (Irénée's father) that in 1800, Napoleon had signed a secret treaty with Spain for control of New Orleans and the surrounding territory. This was alarming to Jefferson, who regarded du Pont as a dear friend and considered France to be the strongest and most strategically aligned ally of the U.S. But nobody who controlled New Orleans could be counted on as a loyal friend of the U.S., because 37% of the U.S. economy passed through the port of New Orleans. In an 1802 letter to Robert Livingston, the U.S. ambassador to France, Jefferson projected that half the U.S. population and half of all agricultural production would soon come from the French-controlled Louisiana territory.[16] Jefferson wanted to buy the land, but his political opponents (including Irénée's own lawyer, Alexander Hamilton) were against it. Napoleon couldn't be trusted, and France owed the U.S. FF18 million. Yet Livingston had made no progress on this problem in a year.

Pierre du Pont had social capital that Livingston lacked. Pierre had assembled the world's best social network of French government ministers and other influencers needed to support a treaty with the U.S.. Joseph Frazier-Hall's Pulitzer-prize nominated biography of the du Pont family describes how Jefferson deployed Pierre du Pont to Paris on a secret mission to secure an agreement. In back-channel diplomacy, Pierre convinced cash-starved France that Jefferson would offer cash and cancel her debt in return for New Orleans and all its territories to the north and west. In a letter to the U.S. military, Jefferson described this in detail and commended Pierre for invaluable service to his new country. Jefferson also asked that an order for gunpowder be put in immediately to Irénée's startup company, I.E. du Pont de Nemours & Cie. That first order for 22,000 pounds of black powder was booked as $10,000 in revenue, roughly half Irénée's first year earnings when the company was desperate for cash. Pierre had converted his social capital to financial capital.

Social capital is real, but it can be difficult to value, since it comes in two forms: realized (spent) and unrealized (stored), and since its durability is highly variable. You can transfer social capital from one person (or gear in the system) to another. How that's done is more art than science.

Intellectual capital is the intellectual property (IP), personal know-how, and expertise that you and your family members possess. If your cousin invents or designs a product that you produce, you're making use of her intellectual capital. As a group, your family enterprise can manage its intellectual capital to generate more financial assets. Lifelong learning is the Future-Forward mindset you need to develop for growing intellectual capital in the family.

IP has important commercial value worldwide. Patents, trademarks, and copyright are all examples of protections available for intellectual capital. Think of them as storage boxes that preserve the value of the intellectual capital over a specified period of time. Or as a ringfence around your markets to keep competitors out. Like Corning, Du Pont has a robust patent history stretching back into the 19th century. And family members themselves were among the patent holders. For example, Irénée's grandson Eugene filed two patent applications in 1889, one for process (the gunpowder press) and one for product (a kind of gunpowder called brown prismatic). Famous du Pont patented products include Lycra, Teflon, Kevlar, and Neoprene.

Driving Your Quantum Machine with the Four Capitals

In the evolving family ecosphere, much of the family enterprise work now involves choosing what kind of resources to power your strategy with—how much of those resources to add—and when.

Working with Financial Capital: Constantly assess how much of the current cash flow generated by your family organizations (or gears) can be devoted to innovation—and how much additional capital will be needed. There may be an array of future opportunities you are preparing, some that will reach financial harvesting in ten, fifteen, twenty, thirty years. Because of this, cash flow becomes the lifeblood of supplying your future endeavors. Make sure you have good family and non-family talent in the family enterprise working as skilled financial analysts.

Short-term projects promising quick returns on financial capital (say, in two to five years) are also important. They let you increase your capital base. It is also wise to consider working with co-investors. They have financial capital you can gear in. A co-investor network of long-term capital partners is invaluable for diversifying risks, entering new industries, and breaking into new geographic markets.

Family ecospheres secure their enduring advantage by converting today's financial capital into talent, social networks, and IP, with the patience to wait til these investments pay off. Your "secret sauce" is in knowing how to make savvy investments for people to thrive.

Working with Human Capital: Following the lead of Corning and many others, innovative organizations always seek the best talent they can afford in the critical aspect of their work. Your family enterprise should do the same. The remainder of this book is devoted to concrete strategies for developing next generation members so they can rise to lead your quantum projects.

Working with Intellectual Capital: What you're aiming for is engaging experts in your family ecosphere who possess unique know-how. As the du Pont case illustrates, if you don't have core family talent right now for the innovations you have committed to, you can acquire that expertise from the inside (scan your gears) or from the outside (scan your social and professional networks).

Working with Social Capital: Networks will be important in establishing and serving global markets for your future innovations. To develop these, start joint initiatives with your trusted partners, other business families, companies, or social enterprises that help "get you out there," building the family brand in new markets, communicating the family mission, and burnishing the family's reputation.

An example of a family enterprise strategy that make primary use of social capital is Rockefeller. The design of Rockefeller Center, a complex of commercial buildings that spanned several city blocks of family property in midtown Manhattan, was undertaken for philanthropic purposes. There was no existing business relationship or current mutual interest that could have brought the parties together; it was the vision of second generation leader, John D. Rockefeller, Jr., that united the key players. Rockefeller developed the innovative land use strategy so that his family could donate land that it leased from Columbia University to the Metropolitan Opera, enabling the charitable organization to raise money for building an opera house. The land development turned into a quantum wealth generator for Rockefeller, his siblings, and all family members of that generation.[17]

Conclusion

Now that you can see the value of Longevity DNA in preparing and harvesting future opportunities, it's time to start evolving your family ecosphere, nurture and build a Future-Forward culture, spot and develop your family talent, and build your Quantum Machine. The rest of this book takes you through those steps.

The most important thing you can do right away to implant Longevity DNA in your family members is to make an action plan and commit resources for innovations that can be harvested in the future. Future-Forward families, and all organizations intent on innovation for quantum impact, need to commit. It's only when you have skin in the game that you will have standing and a voice to shape future conversations that will impact your ecosphere.

CHAPTER 3

Phoenix Rising:
Traits of Exceptional Leadership

Exceptional leaders do the heavy lifting to build great cultures in distributed organizations.

The good news about centerprising leaders is that with them, you can keep your organization thriving into the next generation and beyond. The bad news is, if you can't discover them and nurture them, your organization will wither. As you learned in Chapter 1, cultivating human capital is so important to your success from generation to generation that you must learn to do it well. Good leadership is how you channel the resources to make investments for people to thrive. Good leadership strengthens your core with family unity. It's the key to your enduring advantage.

So, let's begin by reviewing leadership challeges today so we can start building profiles of leaders you need.

You already know, from your own career and other life experiences, that no two leaders are alike. They all have their own ways of solving problems. Everybody has their own style. Leaders develop their unique perspectives.

Take Steve Jobs. He was widely seen as an autocratic leader, always challenging his team to think bigger and better. With his legendary attention to detail, he inspired his team to create world-beating products.[1]

Bill Gates is more of a transactional leader. That means he's task-oriented (even a task master, some would say) with a flair for execution. He doesn't let much stand in the way of accomplishing his agenda.[2]

Co-founders Sergei Brin and Larry Page have led great culture building at Google, consistently named in reputable rankings among America's top tech companies to work for.[3] Building a great culture in distributed organizations is exceedingly hard. At Google, employees are very talented with great ideas of their own. They need to be expertly led in the same direction, rather than managed with inflexibility. Fail, and productivity tumbles. Succeed, and the leader earns employee respect for life.[4] And the company experiences quantum growth.

So, no two leaders in your family organization will be exactly alike. Nor should they be, because each leader develops in their own context with respect to industry, size of organization, regional or national culture, and much more. Every leader has unique passions. They have different strengths and weaknesses. The most important thing to recognize is that leaders have different personalities. Don't blind yourself to the leaders you need by imposing your own biases.

The Centerprising Leadership Traits You Want and Need

Looking around you, it's easy to see that families also have their own style, just as leaders do, with as many differences as commonalities. The same is true of family enterprise. So, you can expect centerprising leaders to be very different types of people. But from my experience advising business families, I see that there's a set of basic qualities that all family business leaders need to possess for them to succeed in their roles.

Family Elders, it's primarily your job to learn how to identify and nurture rising leaders who demonstrate clarity of purpose; can make difficult decisions and exercise good judgment; can inspire and motivate those around them; who exhibit courage; and who can not only chart a path to achieve shared goals, but lead the group to that desired outcome.

Rising leaders, your enterprising family's long-term survival depends on performing above average. That applies to leadership too. There's no such thing as a "good enough" leader. You can always benefit from key learning points to help you become the best that you can be.

Let's explore the roles and responsibilities of a centerprising leader and take a look at common traits that will tell us what a successful leader looks like.

Leadership Challenges Today

Both leaders and followers have roles to play. They're both performing from a script, often called a social contract. This isn't about politics. It's about the implicit agreement that followers are willing to be led. In order for that social contract to work, the followers need to feel that their leader is able to create plans beneficial to them. Followers need confidence in their leaders. They've got to feel certain that leaders can bring them along and achieve their plans. Leaders need to be responsive to changing needs. They also need to recognize how followers signal buy-in before cooperating—or not. In other words, followers have as much power as leaders.

Mandate to lead

Hierarchy has given way to flatter organizational structures. It's easy to see why the most sought-after leaders today govern by collaboration and influence. This approach is well suited to the rise of the sharing economy. It is the crown jewel of the millennial generation still shaping today's youth culture. So, a company that clings to hierarchical, command style leadership will soon find it hard to recruit and retain the best talent.

Few organizations are immune to dramatic changes sweeping the economy. Few industries can hide from firece global competition. Large companies are getting larger, some with near monopoly status. They have the imperative to do the right thing for their stakeholders—employees, clients, surrounding communities, as well as owners—not because they are forced to do so by law or for profit, but for their long-term survival. If you think that's an exaggeration, consider that in most marketplaces around the world, every customer has a smart phone with a camera and a microphone—and so does every critic.

Inside the family, the collaborative leader who leads by moral authority, role modeling, and cultivating others to perform tends to be effective. As discussed in Chapter 2, all Four Capitals (financial, human, intellectual, and social) are important to multigenerational success. Every family member has a reserve of some or all of these resources. By engaging with each individual family member to learn what is important to them, the family leader can channel those resources into the family enterprise and create the force multiplier effect. When family business leaders cannot master this aspect of the job under stress, it usually damages the whole family enterprise, sometimes beyond repair.

Consider the case of a multigenerational business family that might lose control of its legendary, flagship company in a downturn. The company logo bears the family name. The share price is depressed. So why hasn't a financial strategy been adopted to reassure public shareholders and the capital markets?

Looking closer, it becomes clear that the current business leader and controlling owners at the core have overlooked a powerful resource on the edge. One family member, an executive in the company who is highly respected in the industry, has inherited significant wealth outside the business family. But he has never been given a significant business leadership role. So he will never get shareholder approval to succeed the current business leader as CEO in the public company.

To address this problem, the current business leader may have overlooked a potential solution that lies inside the family circle. Longevity DNA can play a role in solving this problem. Because of the intense pride and fierce loyalty that motivates the wealthy family executive, he might be persuaded to accept the Co-Chairman role in return for buying a major block of shares to maintain family control. If that happened, it would be a quantum effect of the Longevity DNA that has been nurtured in this family for generations.[5]

Governance roles

Industries are changing at such speed that legal frameworks and government processes struggle to keep up. In the A.I. (artificial intelligence) and blockchain spaces, frameworks for self-governance are being suggested that would involve the scientific community, leading companies, and other stakeholders. Whether the major players resist innvations in self-governance or adopt them, this is a sign of things to come.

Seasoned leaders know that it's a new world where business leaders, not just governmental leaders, will soon need the social mandate to lead. A world where family companies must have a strong moral core to be authentic and to be accepted by the communities they profit from.

Driving this shift in leadership dynamics are global demographics. We see large business organizations with ever-younger CEOs at the helm. Naturally, there are pitfalls with younger leaders. They may grasp technical systems and hardware better, but do you trust them to do the right thing? Their lack of life experience can lead the company into trouble. The fall of Uber's co-founder Travis Kalanick is one example of youthful hubris. When problems at the company came to a head in 2017, Kalanick, at forty, was considered an experienced leader, almost an "elder statesman" in Silicon Valley.[6] Then came accusations that he fostered a toxic culture and turned a blind eye to reports of sexual harassment at Uber. It led to his resignation by the end of the year.[7] Good leaders take time to develop, not just for the purpose of advancing their skills but also to deepen their moral discernment and exercise good judgment.

Versatility and cultural sensitivity

Versatility is also becoming a critical leadership quality. It has always been true to say that a successful leader will face many different types of situations over the span of their career. In our increasingly globalized world, leaders must immediately confront the limits of their native styles and norms, and then also be willing and able to adapt.

Different cultures will always nurture different kinds of leaders. For example, the model leader in China is often portrayed in movies as a fatherly figure, a paternalistic influence on business and culture. In times of trouble, he is expected to "go down with the ship." The reasoning goes that he should save others before saving himself, sacrificing himself in a crisis for the common good. His focus is on tomorrow. In the West, however, the model leader is often a hero focused on today who saves the day and survives at all costs.

The path a leader takes toward any trusted decision depends on the context, too. In the U.S., a business leader "makes a decision" at a meeting, where buy-in can be attained at the same time. Public buy-in and timeliness are what Americans value and trust most highly. In Europe, the leader "takes a decision" after the meeting, getting the buy-in he or she needs in private among key influencers. That method is more highly valued and trusted in many European cultures. In East Asia, decisions made among strangers are usually not regarded very highly. It is important for Western leaders to invest significant time and other resources in building relationships before coming to a trusted decision when working with Asian partners in the Eastern context. This slows down the process, which can hurt a Western leader's reputation for decisiveness in their home context. The global family business leader of today must have the skill to make decisions and gain trust in multiple cultural contexts, which adds to the complexity of their decision-making process.

Today's successful leader may operate out of several geographical bases. The leader travels a lot. Wherever they wake up on any given day, they know how to tap into the culture around them. The leader has a firm grasp of their moral compass in that society. He or she understands the influences of education, law, religion, philosophy, and other factors in constructing the accepted norms. The French have a simple and useful way of indicating this capability when they refer to somebody as "well brought up" (*bien élevé*) and "cultivated" (*cultivé*). In the U.S., liberal arts colleges champion a similar ideal of the "Renaissance person," distinguished by their broad and creative intellect. These qualities are important in building social capital, which is why they still characterize successful leaders.

Cultural sensitivity is especially important for the leader who needs to provide oversight over global businesses and build unity within a global family group. Consider a family group with branches in America, Europe, and Asia that includes interracial marriages, plus cousins who grew up speaking different native languages and being exposed to different cultures. This is increasingly the reality of large, successful multigenerational business families. Followers need to know that leaders are comfortable in the followers' context.

So, to summarize, here are four qualities of exceptional leaders:

1. *Good judgment*—knowing how and when to make a decision.

2. *Moral authority*—acting and deciding based on knowing right from wrong.

3. *Building trusted relationships*—behaving consistently and keeping your word.

4. *Character and attitude*—having persistence, curiosity, versatility, cultural sensitivity, an entrepreneurial spirit, and the fortitude and boldness to take big, calculated risks.

Leaders You Need

To centerprise successfully, you often need more than one type of leader. Broadly speaking, at least three common types of leaders are needed in a typical family enterprise:

1. *Business leaders* who oversee the growth of family resources and make meaningful financial investments for people to thrive;

2. *The family leader* who manages family governance, talent development of all family members, and conflicts among family members as they relate to the family enterprise; and

3. *Social entrepreneurs* who lead and coordinate the family's overall efforts for doing good in communities.

Each of these leaders needs to have a spike in a certain skill area. *Business leaders* must be business savvy, able to spot opportunities, and aware of the changing nature and value of the resources you possess. They need to have a strategic mindset. They don't need a full time senior management role; they can be non-executive chairman. They should be versed in finance and accounting, strategy, and have some general understanding of all other areas related to running a business such as marketing, sales, legal, IT, and/or manufacturing as applicable. The biggest challenge in selecting and cultivating business leaders is that the business itself is a moving target. Our world is changing so quickly, the business landscape in ten years' time will surely be very different from what it is today. A traditional "up-the-ladder" training program may or may not be the best approach. So, keep an open mind and focus on the rising leader's level of curiosity, willingness to learn, and problem-solving skills.

Family leaders are individuals who work to support family unity by (1) being active in the family governance structure (e.g., family council), (2) engaging with each family member individually, and (3) developing the next generation family group. They may also lead the agenda of the family owners. Family leaders can be the business leaders, but as business families evolve, they tend to be well-respected family members who do not hold formal roles in the wealth engines. Their responsibilities may include oversight of annual distributions; family employment policy; hiring and firing of a family CEO; compensation or perks for family managers; and the future direction of the family's wealth engines. The family leaders have a very important role in family enterprises transforming into an ecosphere by building a Quantum Machine that creates a multiplier impact from the family's collective resources. These leaders need to focus on (and become skilled at) developing and engaging every family member.

Social entrepreneurs may be involved with the family foundation or institution, non-profits, impact investing, or other community activities focused on doing good. They are the family's face in
the communities. Families whose wealth engines and social entrepreneurs coordinate on some levels often experience a multiplier
impact in both areas.

Performance versus success

Even though each leadership type has its own distinct set of characteristics, they share some commonalities. Let's explore the commonalities for now.

First, let's take a look at the terminology. The terms "trait" and
"skill set" are often used interchangeably, as are "performance" and
"success." These concepts are closely linked, but there are subtle yet
important differences between them.

Traits are characteristics that an effective leader should possess.
They include self-awareness, boldness, and decisiveness. Traits are
linked to personalities. We all possess innate tendencies toward
certain traits, such as shyness or sociability. Some traits, like sociability, can be cultivated with practice, muscle memory, and mindset
shift. But other traits, such as boldness, are difficult to instill. In the
face of battle, very few people have nerves of steel when most others retreat in haste. No matter how you train them, it is difficult to
predict with high certainty how a person who is not innately bold
will behave at critical moments of high stress.

Skill sets are capabilities or abilities that a person learns. Level
of skills mastery depends on both innate talent and hard work.
Alex Honnold is the world's top rock climber at the age of thirty-
three, the only person who has ever free soloed the 3,000 foot cliff
El Capitan in California's Yosemite valley. Adding to his mastery
on monumental, "big wall" routes is Honnold's monumental persistence. Preparing for the El Cap climb, Honnold trained with a
belay partner for more than a year, ascending with ropes over fifty
times, committing each move on his almost four-hour journey to
memory.[8] Passion and discipline combine in Honnold's Herculean
work ethic.

Performance is more than winning. In leaders, it's delivering
results over and over again under ever-changing circumstances.
Think of a Grand Slam tennis champion, who must deliver high performance on multiple court surfaces, day in and day out, around the

world. Performance is a measure of how well a leader applies all of her favorable skill sets and traits in a specific context (and suppresses her non-favorable traits for that context), in order to design, lead, and execute an initiative to achieve a good outcome. This often requires inspiring and mobilizing followers in the face of one or more challenges. Plus, spotting any constraints and opportunities that exist.

Success is whether the outcome is favorable. It often hinges on luck and is not always under the control of the leader. Luck plays an important role in the success of any enterprise and its leader. We want leaders to learn, understand, and appreciate the role of luck. When we see a successful leader, chances are that he has been both fortunate and skillful.

Take Bill Gates. In *Outliers*, Malcolm Gladwell focuses on the role that good fortune played in Gate's development. "He has this extraordinary string of lucky breaks," Gladwell said later, "starting with the fact that in 1969 he gets access to a computer terminal and is able to do computing in real time at the age of 13, for almost as much time as he wanted. Now, the number of people who had the opportunity in 1969 who were teenagers in the world ... you know, as Bill Gates said, if it was 50 he'd be stunned."[9] Interviewed about this by his father shortly after the book was published, Gates said: "In all success stories, there are significant elements of luck and timing."[10] Billionaire investor Howard Marks, co-founder of Oak Tree Capital Management writes: "We all know that when things go right, luck looks like skill."[11] But whether your luck is good or bad, it cannot account for every outcome.

In his 2018 TED talk, Alex Honnold compared his free solo climb of Yosemite's 2,000 foot Half Dome with the 3,000 foot ascent of El Capitan. The Half Dome climb was unsatisfying, he said, because he was unprepared. Honnold had left it up to luck to accomplish it successfully. The climb of El Capitan was, by contrast, meticulously prepared. This was where Honnold could prove to himself that he was a high performer. The successful outcome gave him enormous satisfaction.[12]

Even if you have a strong work ethic, performance depends on skills and traits, while success requires both great performance and good luck. Leaders who are viewed by others as successful typically project a mix of humility and pride because they appreciate the luck involved.

Focusing on success is an obsession for many managers today. But it can be a path to disappointment because you cannot turn luck on and off like a water faucet. Instead, I suggest that family enterprises focus on whether the leader is effective: demonstrating high performance by taking the right steps in any given context, using the skills and traits that are required in that situation.

Centerpriser: Portrait of an Effective Family Organization Leader

So, what does a great family organization leader look like? Centered, anchored, and innovating. He or she embraces their family enterprise's core values and believes in supporting the family enterprise to survive and thrive in the long term, which means cultivating all four essential capitals (financial, human, intellectual, and social). The effective leader has a Future-Forward mindset and deeply understands how innovation on the edge and adaptation at the core are key to survival. To be better than average is to thrive, and the leader knows that thriving, for the whole system or ecosphere, is not just keeping up with the times, but making sure the entire next generation gets engaged and stays engaged.

By definition, the leader works in the the family organization–whether as a business leader, family leader, or social entrepreneur. He or she takes an inclusive stance, encouraging a big tent attitude that supports family talent and passions of all kinds. It's not just business talent that needs support. It's all the talent needed to grow the Four Capitals. The leader devotes fiscal and other resources to that goal, too. He or she is dedicated to maintaining a culture of evolving the core values for tomorrow, yet protecting their integrity today.

John Elkann, leading the Agnelli family organization that owns the Italian auto maker Fiat, is a master at this. In personality, he strikes a balance between projecting hard-nosed, business sense and exuding familial warmth. Under his guidance, there is a porousness in the system that engages positive outside influences, but not so much openness as to bring instability to the core. That would undermine the integrity that has enabled the family to thrive for generations. Elkann is a skilled centerpriser.

The grandson of the founder, Elkann joined the boards of the Fiat Group and its parent company IFI (later restructured as Exor) at the age of twenty-one, replacing his mother's cousin Giovanni, who had died unexpectedly. Even the best laid plans go awry, and succession can catch a family unawares. Seven years later, Elkann was only twenty-eight when he was appointed Vice-Chairman of Fiat and thrust into the leadership role at Exor after the deaths of his grandfather and great-uncle. He had been born into what has often been described as "Italian industrial royalty," and had worked in the business after university, but Elkann never expected to become head of the business family. In 2010, still only 34, Elkann became Chairman of Fiat; a year later, he took on the roles of Chairman and CEO of Exor.

At the time of Elkann's succession, Fiat had cycled through four CEOs in three years and was approaching bankruptcy. Clearly, it needed a strong and experienced leader to pull it out of this morass. Many expected that the task would prove too great for Elkann. But from the outset, he was decisive and innovative to a degree that surprised many observers. Defying expectations, he modernized the company and renewed its assets, taking a bold position that proved successful. Elkann agreed to dilute the Agnelli family stake in order to pave the way for the company to acquire 20% of Chrysler in 2009, and later led a demerger of the group. "John took a very modern approach to the portfolio," says David Herro, chief investment officer of Harris Associates, which owns 7.3% of Exor. "What often happens in these things is that people get attached to certain assets, [but] John did away with any kind of legacy loyalty."[13] These deals, each involving some loss of control, were unthinkable for previous generations, and even shocked other European car making families, such as the Peugeots. However, the Agnelli family reaped the rewards in the subsequent share price rise.[14]

The leader's steep learning curve had paid off, both in terms of business outcomes and personal rewards. "My biggest satisfaction was to learn, inexperienced as I was, that it is possible to find ways out of the deepest difficulties," says Elkann. "I learnt not to be desperate in bad times and am learning not to be bullish when times are good."[15]

How to Be an Exceptional Leader

Does it seem massively challenging to become the kind of multignerational enterprise leader that you aspire to be? It won't be easy. But that doesn't mean it has to be complex. Basically, you need to possess or acquire three key qualities.

Key Learning Point #1: Develop your *self-awareness*. Understand yourself as a leader, along with your strengths and weaknesses. Use your strengths well to further your family enterprise's goals; make up shortcomings by improving on those leadership skills or find someone with a complementary skillset whom you can work with.

Key Learning Point #2: Seek to *develop your sensitivity* to different contexts: the kind of cultural, emotional, educational, and functional circumstances that may shape your colleagues' thinking. This "pool" of influences will determine how motivated others are to embrace your leadership. Be mindful of particular fears, in yourself and in others, that may make people resistant to following your direction.

Key Learning Point #3: *Widen the range* of your leadership skills by learning how to interact with people in different "microcontexts." For example, a family organization leader might need to negotiate highly technical contracts with corporate lawyers, while also being able to lead collective bargaining with union workers, where the tenor of communications is completely different.

Key Learning Point #4: *Exercise good judgment* in terms of selecting key hires to fill your team and play roles in key decisions.

How to Measure a Leader

A successful leader is in control: she may be guiding the family enterprise overall with multiple capital resources that she is juggling at once, or she may be guiding a part of the family enterprise focused on developing one or two types of capital. She is constantly taking stock of these resources and knows how, where, and when to use them. She also has a handle on when to develop more of each resource (financial, social, human, or intellectual). In summary, she is good at developing and allocating capital.

Above all, the effective family enterprise leader is the one leading a healthy, personally fulfilled life with psychological balance. Without such equilibrium, leaders do not have the stamina to serve for long periods, or the ability to make measured, thoughtful decisions in challenging circumstances.

Conclusion

For your family business to survive and thrive in the long term, few considerations are as significant as the quality of the leaders you cultivate. If your leadership team has all of the centerprising attributes—anchored, innovative, and talent development focused— then your family enterprise is well placed to be at the forefront of your industry and the global community.

CHAPTER 4

Survival Hacks:
Resolving Generational Tensions

Founders can walk through fire. But they can't see what motivates their kids.

To an outside onlooker, Joe[1] has an enviable life. He is the son of a leading business founder with a senior management position in the family company. His colleague Daniel, on the other hand, has worked hard to reach his current role as an investment manager in the single family office set up by Joe's father. Daniel is not a family member. Joe and Daniel come from different backgrounds, but they like spending time together.

One morning over coffee, Daniel tells Joe that he'll soon be leaving the family office to start his own investment fund. Joe is delighted for his colleague, even though he feels a twinge of envy. He would love to stretch his wings independently from his family. Joe believes he could achieve more if only he could get out from under his father's somewhat intimidating shadow. But Joe's sense of duty to his family is strong, and he feels compelled to stay. All the same, he can't shake the feeling that he doesn't have control over anything in his work or personal life because his dad pays his salary.

As Joe walks back to his office, he thinks that he would willingly trade places with Daniel. Joe's path takes him past his father's office. He slows down. The door is shut. Joe considers knocking but moves on. His father is very busy with important matters, and it seems inappropriate to bother him. Besides, Joe has no idea how he would share these feelings with his father. He's never done it before.

Consider this scene from the viewpoint of the founder's executive assistant, watching Joe walk past his father's door. To her and to most people, Joe's path looks like it's lined with roses. But along with the sweet fragrance comes a thorn or two. Founders and their offspring may be connected by blood and familial loyalty, but they could not be more different in critical ways. A wide gap in interests, attitudes, and mentality arise out of their very different life experiences. Founders often start with nothing, so they can afford to risk losing everything. In contrast, successors start with accumulated wealth and are deathly afraid to lose it.

In my work with leading family enterprises in various industries spread across different geographies, I have observed common challenges faced by all rising leaders. These challenges are rooted in generational conflicts. There are six of these generational tensions that need to be addressed, otherwise talent development is doomed to fail.

Tension One: To Fail or Not to Fail?

Founders, you have walked through fire. You probably started with no money, met with multiple failures, and—oh, remember the time that your former business partner started a competing firm and forced your company to fold? You had to start all over, building from the ground up. These are the tests that forge founders in steel by circumstance.

You tend to feel confident that you can navigate any adversity and overcome any challenge. In stark contrast, the leader who will follow you grew up untested by financial stress. The seasoned wealth creator is everyone's role model for success, but it is one tough act to follow. Rising leaders experience a unique set of fears that are entirely foreign to the proven wealth creators. Rising family leaders are terrified of being the ones to lose the family fortune through their own missteps. As a result, they can be highly risk averse.

All founders, therefore, should build a culture that embraces thoughtful failure. Family elders, consider being the champion of this culture. Give everyone permission to fail smartly. Advise the next generation to calculate the risks before acting; do a post-mortem after experiencing failure; extract key lessons; and help them make sure they don't fail the same way twice.

Current stewards should teach future stewards that what matters most is not hitting a home run every time, or even making money every time, but developing the ability to take calculated risks. You should expect some wins and some losses. Success is defined by a few significant wins that outweigh all the smaller losses. With that macro-perspective, the rising leader will be encouraged to experiment and will learn, over time, not to be afraid of failing at any specific project, because they will have the bigger picture in their sights.

Tension Two: "I Need to Be Me"

Being known as the "son or daughter of XX" or "that rich kid" can be a heavy load to carry. Every new generation sees the senior leaders as towering giants of accomplishment, and that can be daunting. Rising leaders often feel that they're coming up short when measured against their elders. Did you feel that way when you were young, looking up at your patriarch? Did you have to struggle to step out from his shadow and establish your own distinct identity and credibility? Think back to those times, and you will have more empathy for your rising generation. A rising leader usually has to become their own person before they willingly engage with the family legacy and lead it through renewal—or even better, rebirth.

While rebelliously shaping their distinct identity, rising leaders also look for validation from their ultra-successful seniors. Thomas Watson Jr., the son of the founder of IBM, who became the second CEO of the company, wrote this in the introduction to his memoir:

> While I was chief executive [for fifteen years] the company grew more than tenfold. I'd like to think that Father would have been impressed with the $7.5 billion-a-year business I left behind when I resigned in 1971 … I had a compelling desire, maybe out of honor for the old gentleman, maybe out of sheer cussedness, to prove to the world that I could excel the same way he did.[2]

This internal tension, spurred by the age-old conflict of youth versus experience, is what many rising leaders struggle with. It can create real conflict between parents and children in the family enterprise. Can you, seniors, be more sensitive to their internal struggles? It would benefit them greatly.

Tension Three: Internal Drive—Can the Monster Be Awakened?

Seasoned leaders, do you remember feeling that incredible "fire in the belly" when you were young that just said to you, "I have to succeed, no matter what challenges are thrown at me"? Today, do you have this nagging feeling that none of your rising leaders is hungry enough to become a breakout success? Maybe you even feel that way about the whole next generation. Look at it from their perspective.

A lifetime of material needs were met the day they were born into the business family. Why should they work hard? Or risk conflict by introducing new ideas into the family company that are likely to be beaten down? Travel or even move house and home to manage factories in remote areas? Why should they cloud over their comfortable lifestyle with concerns about the family company?

Seniors, if you really want to attract your offspring with prospects of taking over the company, why are you constantly telling them what to do, criticizing them, and making them feel inadequate? This is not very persuasive.

Most proven wealth creators (especially founders) have been driven by fear of poverty, resentment over low status, or a strong desire to excel. These motivators were always there on the surface. Rising leaders have to dig deep inside for motivation. They usually end up asking themselves, "What is the purpose of my life?" Questions of personal meaning and life purpose are more complex for the emerging generation, because they really do have more choices. Wealth gives them these choices. To reach fulfillment, rising family leaders need to find their True North and connect that with the strategic needs of the family enterprise. Successors need to awaken their internal drive to unleash their own creativity and that of the family enterprise, leading the system to rebirth. This is a different destiny from the founder's destiny. To reach it, successors will follow a different path.

In his book *Drive: The Surprising Truth of What Motivates Us*, Daniel Pink[3] sets out three key factors that make for effective internal motivation:

1. *Autonomy.* Our desire to be self-directed. It increases engagement over compliance.

2. *Mastery.* The drive to acquire better skills.

3. *Purpose.* The desire to do something that has meaning and is important.

Business leaders who put too much emphasis on profits without valuing purpose are more likely to end up with unhappy customers and disgruntled employees. People aspire to greater things. Every rising leader needs to find his purpose and to connect it to that of the family business.

Strongest motivations come from within, not from without. A leader's desire for fulfillment will almost always outweigh any material incentive, whether positive (such as a reward) or negative (such as a punishment).

Let's consider what happens when seniors threaten to take away inheritance or financial support. One or more members of the rising generation will either rebel completely, leading to estrangement, or else they will be obedient yet not deliver anything above and beyond what is asked of them—not the behavior of a future leader. And you've lost talent along the way, which you can't afford either.

Pride in accomplishments, overcoming the odds against you, conquering fear or shame, rebounding after setbacks, doing good, making a difference: these are the motivators that have real impact.

Tension Four: Set Aside Your Internal Dictator

Like Joe, whom we met at the beginning of this chapter, many successors complain that they have no control over their own lives because their future path has already been planned by their seniors. They feel their wings are clipped. And they reason that they have no decision-making authority in their lives and their work.

To dispel this cloud, it's best for seniors to influence their family's future talent by stepping in to guide them at a young age when they're open to it. As children and young people grow into adulthood, seasoned leaders should shift the strategy and focus on centerprising—providing opportunities and support to rising family members in their chosen endeavors. Above all, it's critical *not to dictate* the rising generation's future plans. That is one practice that's almost guaranteed to backfire. As the head of their companies, senior business leaders who reached the height of their careers in the late 20th century may still have a default setting in "hierarchical mode." Not only have social norms changed in the workplace, because of the shift to flatter organizations, but modern family dynamics don't allow you to engage in "command mode."

When elders ask me, "How can I develop my next generation?" I suggest this: do it in your parental role, not in the senior executive role you take on when managing employees. This often requires a dramatic shift in behavior, not just in strategy, outlook, or demeanor. With time and practice, you'll start to see the results you're looking for. Remember Anderson and Alexandre Birman, the father-son team at Arezzo? They train for sports competitions together. It's an ideal example of Anderson's seasoned leadership skills.

Tension Five: Finding Common Ground with Millennials

What about the cultural differences that patriarchs, matriarchs and their successors are experiencing around the world? Don't generation gaps come in different international flavors? Maybe that was true before. Today, not so much. Members of the millennial generation born between 1981 and 1996, according to the Pew Research Center, are vastly more similar to each other worldwide than we've ever seen before—and they're starkly different from members of other generations.[4] This shared culture among millennials globally is driven by the digital revolution that reinforces cultural similarities throughout the connected world. Millennial attitudes toward the value of time, like putting a high value on achieving better work–life balance and focusing on getting the work done, rather than "wasting" face time, tend to frustrate the senior generation. There seems to be less overlap of values between the generations than in previous decades. Because of this, it's much more important than ever before to practice good communication about shared goals and methods for achieving them. Millennials like more responsibility earlier. They like more feedback frequently. And they like being recognized for a job well done when deserved.

Another generational difference is in convictions. Millennials place higher value on working for the common good. This is a natural consequence of growing up in a relatively plentiful and peaceful era, without memories of the Cold War and the multitudes of regional wars and global threats that stemmed from it. As far as most millennials are concerned, doing good is good business, and it was a sign of the times in 2018 when Forbes launched its Just 100 list to rank companies that build success on principles of enlightened leadership.[5] There are well-tested ways for family enterprises to do well by doing good that both generations can explore and design together. In 2011, economist Michael Porter, the guru of competitive advantage from the Harvard Business School, introduced the concept of Creating Shared Value, explaining how companies can create measurable business value by identifying and addressing social problems that intersect with their business.[6] Mikkel Vestergaard-Frandsen's innovation strategy at Vestergaard, the Swiss health products company he founded that transformed his Danish family business, is a classic example of shared value principles at work.

China, in particular, must reckon with an additional driver that widens the gap between generations. Most Chinese founders, especially those who started their businesses in the first wave of economic reforms during the 1980s, did not study outside of China. Given their age and the culture in which they grew up, the hierarchical, top-down way of doing things is deeply ingrained. A large percentage of their children, however, have had some education abroad and have been influenced by Western values. As a result, the emerging generation often has different views on matters such as business strategy, the use of capital, organizational structure, delegation, and decision-making processes. So there isn't just a generation gap between Chinese millennials and their seniors. There's a cultural gap too. This can make for extremely challenging communication between the generations, possibly imperiling a generation of family companies in China.

Tension Six: Whose Vision Will Win Out?

Current leaders and their successors often have different perspectives on the future development of industries. They need to create consensus to be able to work toward a common goal. Or at least, one party has to be convinced enough of the vision, and have enough confidence in the other party's ability to execute, to be supportive of the overall strategic evolution of the family company.

Thomas Watson Jr. described his struggles with his dad to create a new company vision this way:

> In private, Father and I had terrible fights that led us again and again to the brink of estrangement. These arguments would frequently end in tears, me in tears and Dad in tears. We fought about every major issue of the business—how to finance IBM's growth, whether to settle or fight a federal anti-trust suit, what role in IBM other members of our family ought to play. From around 1950 my goal—one of the things on which we never saw eye to eye—was to push into computers as fast as possible ... When I finally took over, I was excited about change. Computing was a brand-new industry, and I always felt that if IBM didn't grab the opportunity, someone else would.[7]

It was IBM's pivot into computers that allowed it to grow ten times in the 15 years that Thomas Watson Jr. was CEO.

This process of vision alignment is often difficult—filled with unending conflict and heavy emotional burden among elders and their successor(s). But the hard work pays off when the rising leader becomes the steady hand at the helm after constant challenges by the preceding generation. These life lessons are best learned through struggling with real life business problems in real time, and with open debates between the two generations. In the end, this is apt to produce a confident leader who is open to consider others' opinions and then be able to make decisive decisions on his own, leading the company toward realizing an ambitious yet achievable goal.

The Secret to Resolving the Six "Tensions"

Add up these six dramatic tensions and it is little wonder that there is conflict between the generations. Rising family leaders want validation and support from their elders, yet at the same time they struggle to define their own unique identity. These opposing forces often result in stormy relationships, especially when next generation members are in their twenties, thirties and forties. All of these friction points can be resolved, but in each area of tension, the process must be addressed slowly, consistently, and patiently. It takes a great deal of time and effort for the patriarch and the successor to reach consensus so that the strength of what has been built is retained and the changes that are needed to keep up with the times can be implemented.

Spotting the Stars

Most family enterprises select a few members of the rising generation to develop and invite into the family enterprise. In the current distributed economy with many technology disruptions where there is a clear war for talent, I would like to suggest that seasoned leaders centerprise and develop all talent in the family pool, primarily because it is difficult to know from early on whether any rising generation member will become a breakout success. Many breakout successors were perceived by their fathers as unremarkable, unmotivated, or even lazy. This was as true of E.I. DuPont in the 18th century as it was of Thomas Watson, Jr. in the 20th. And then there's Billy Vanderbilt, one of history's most successful sons in business.

Billy Vanderbilt was the son of Commodore Cornelius Vanderbilt, the second or third richest person in American history.[8] When he was young, Billy was often berated and criticized by his father as a "blockhead" and a "blatherskite."[9] He later distinguished himself by abandoning the shipping industry his father swore by, and placing huge bets in the emerging railway industry. He inherited almost $100 million from his father in 1877 and had doubled it in nine years by the time of his death in 1885.[10] Not bad for a blockhead.

Welcome to Your Second Career

To maximize the chance of transition success, elders need to evolve their role from being purely a wealth creator to a talent developer. If this sounds like you, get ready for a major challenge. Along with the role shift, a certain amount of humility is required to alter your mentality, how you allocate your time, and how you communicate in the mentor role rather than the executive leadership role. This is what it takes to fortify your connection with the emerging generation. It wouldn't be worth the effort if the rewards weren't so great, taking the form of an enduring family enterprise.

In my advisory work, I see that rising leaders usually crave time spent with the seasoned leader to discuss business and other topics. This stems in part from the desire to receive recognition for her own achievements and validation that her parent has confidence in her. Elders, do you set aside enough time to communicate deeply with the rising generation? Developing regular and effective communication between the two generations is the foundation of successful leadership development.

Effective communication between the founder and the next generation relies on three components:

1. *Schedule regular communication with a clear agenda*, allowing enough time to prepare and to exchange views on issues before making a decision.

2. *Clarify the role you both are assuming in this particular communication.* Are you turning up as CEO, parent, owner, or mentor? Each role brings with it different social expectations. In the CEO role, there are hierarchy and structured

authority, responsibilities, and deadlines to respect. In the parent role, there's only authority—and parental authority relies on trust and understanding to earn respect from adult children. In this role, the elder family member should aim to help guide the rising leader and build their self-confidence. In the ownership role, the conversation may involve making tradeoffs—balancing long-term wealth creation versus short-term distributions to shareholders. Be sure that the emerging generation knows what role you are assuming, and therefore what role they should assume, so they can have the right expectations. Use the tone and approach that is right for that role, and do not mix your roles. If you want to switch roles within one conversation, state that you are doing so in order to avoid confusion. And accept that you may need a follow up conversation, because the cognitive skills required to manage role-switching tend to dampen or repress how we respond to any emotional content. Emotional content in conversations between family members is always just as important as (and sometimes more important than) intellectual content.

3. *Set the right expectations around decision making.* For each decision where you engage the rising generation, be clear with yourself and with them whether (a) you will be making the decision and they are only providing input; (b) the two of you will make the decision together; or (c) the rising leader will make the decision with your input.

Survival Hacks

Rising leaders, this chapter was written for the seniors. If you've made it this far, you've got great survival skills. I admit, the list above can tune out even the most patient reader. While seniors transform themselves to help you succeed, which frankly amounts to a second career, you have some work to do, too.

1. *Be empathetic.* You are high maintenance. Your attention spans are so short that you require master teachers to put all their wisdom in five second sound bytes. You demand messages that are flawlessly produced, ridiculously funny, and Instagrammable so you can share them with the rest of

the world. This is really hard to deal with for anyone who is not a digital native.

2. *Use active listening.* It may freak your parents out, because they are not used to you listening to them. Now is the time. Your parents have been competing against the screen for your attention your whole life. Surprise them.

3. *Stop framing them as old and out of touch.* It only puts up barriers to understanding. Plus, you really do have a lot to learn from them. Wouldn't you want to learn the ropes from Dumbledore? Like Dumbledore, your parents have to live with the burden of knowing where you are likely to make mistakes, and be willing to suffer the heartache of seeing you make them, so that you can learn and grow. They are so dependable, they're boring. They just pored through that boring list above, to soak up every word, so that they can figure out how to interact with you effectively. Your parents have been your protectors for your whole life. And they always will be. Trust in them to have your best interests at heart.

Conclusion

Founders, your life experience has been very different from your successors. It is a major challenge for each generation to understand what motivates the other. Whenever you feel that a successful transition is out of your reach, try to look on the bright side. This gap between you and your successor will narrow over time as you begin to appreciate one another's perspective. The gap between second and third generation leaders will be even narrower. You are still a trailblazer, even at the peak of your career. Hang in there. This work is worth doing well.

As a seasoned leader of a mutigenerational enterprise, there can be few tasks as satisfying as cultivating your successors. Identify what drives your rising leaders, and then build on that by developing their internal motivations. Their engagement will be spurred by desires and aspirations rather than fear and/or guilt. This way, you are in a great position to reap the benefits through the years (and generations) to come, as your rising Phoenixes begin to soar.

Seniors and Rising G: if you think your generational transition is hard, visit centerprising.org to read about the Top 5 Most Chaotic Successions Ever
I predict you'll be writing appreciation letters to each other in no time! Please send copies!

CHAPTER 5

Switch on the Longevity Gene

It's not about wealth or status. It's relationships that keep us fulfilled and productive throughout our lives.

The last word that newspaper magnate Charles Foster Kane ever uttered was "Rosebud."[1] It is widely believed that Kane—the central character in the 1941 film "Citizen Kane"—was referring to the trade name of his childhood sled, which he was playing with just before he was taken away from his family to live with a guardian so that he could get a better education. William Randolph Hearst III, grandson of the publishing tycoon on whom Kane is believed to be based, saw it this way:

> I think there is something sad in the character Kane, and to some degree in my grandfather's personality, that inside that little world it's youth, it's childhood, it's home, it's safe, and they'd like to go back to that. I think that's what Rosebud is. It's really that sense of a childhood denied, in some way.[2]

Why are literature and cinema full of unhappy wealthy kids, growing up emotionally abandoned by their parents? Is this a clue to the childhood roots of adult happiness and health? These are critical questions for those of us who want to cultivate family members capable of raising family leaders. Unfortunately, we can't turn to business books for the answer. Turns out, business leaders rated highest by their peers in emotional intelligence are more likely to read literary fiction.[3]

But there is one place to turn for data. Let me take you on a tour of a small corner of my alma mater, Harvard University, where the world's first major prospective study (one that watches a group of subjects over a long period to see how certain factors affect certain outcomes) has been tracking optimal development for more than seventy-five years.

In 1939, Harvard's Grant study began by assessing the physical and mental well-being of a group of male graduates of Harvard

College. Since then, researchers have followed the lives of 268 men who graduated from 1939 to 1944. Every year, they interviewed the men and asked them to fill out lengthy questionnaires about every aspect of their lives, including their detailed memories of childhood. In parallel, another study tracked a different group: 454 poor men growing up in Boston from 1939 to 2014. This was the Glueck study (pronounced "Glue-eck").[4]

Together, the Glueck and Grant studies comprise the world's longest (and probably most costly) prospective inquiry into holistic human health. Gathering data over seventy-five years on people who scattered to the four corners of the earth after college graduation has been a daunting task.

Why go to all this trouble? The long-time project director George Vaillant and the research team wanted to identify the psychosocial predictors of healthy adult development and aging. The studies' findings are profound and astonishing; some would even say deceptively simple. Both the Grant and Glueck studies confirm that close relationships are what keep people happy and productive throughout their lives. It is intimacy that staves off mental and physical decline. Intimacy proves to be a better indicator of a long and happy life than wealth, fame, class, IQ, or genes.[5]

The Harvard findings support everything that social scientists, biologists, and medical doctors learned about child development in the second half of the twentieth century. Studies confirm that no matter what childrearing philosophy you embrace, the best practices of child development are grounded in the foundation that all human beings need secure relationships for optimal health.

Develop Leaders from the Moment They Are Born

Developing future leaders starts at birth. This is no exaggeration. Using new imaging tools, scientists are unraveling the mystery of how a child goes from being a tiny bundle at birth, unable to grasp a finger, to being able to talk, run, laugh, and make friends by the age of five.[6] The more we learn about how children develop in those early years of life, the more we realize that the newborn brain is a remarkable learning machine. And its future, to a very large degree, is in our hands.

So as adults cultivating rising leaders and innovators, we need to provide newborns and kids under the age of ten with a strong, stable foundation for their learning machines. If we do it right, we will see two major benefits. Our children will grow up emotionally healthy and intellectually curious.[7]

Secure attachment

First, we'll watch the development of a child who enjoys good psychological and emotional health. By being securely attached to one primary caregiver, the child gains self-confidence and learns to trust in others. Just as important, children learn to behave in ways that enable others to trust them. In their book, *Raising a Secure Child,*[8] psychotherapists Kent Hoffman, Glen Cooper, and Bert Powell propose that a secure attachment leads to "confidence and trust in the goodness of me, you, us" that a person carries every day throughout their life. Equipped with the confidence that they are loved and supported no matter what happens, a world of possibilities becomes available to them.

Studies by attachment experts such as John Bowlby and Mary Ainsworth have shown that a securely attached child is usually a curious child.[9] These toddlers and little kids can take the risk of exploring their world, because they know that they can always come back to their anchor (the primary caregiver), who will reliably be there to support them. This healthy curiosity is one of the best qualities that family enterprises should seek to cultivate in their rising generation members, and as you can see, the process starts from the very earliest months of a child's life.

This securely attached, emotionally healthy baby and child is also able to self-sooth and demonstrate self-control. Soon, as researchers have shown in the groundbreaking 2016 study led by a team at Stanford, University of Chicago, and MIT, the small child will be able to explore the world around her with confidence and play on her own. She will be able to engage creatively without constant hovering from caregivers.[10] Daily reinforcements of security lead kids to feel comfortable in their own skin. They're able to form healthy relationships with the people around them, so that they can give and receive love in a fulfilling way.

These securely attached kids are the children who will go on to develop compassion, manage their personal finances responsibly, live within their means, pay their taxes, and be law-abiding citizens. They will respect others and know that money cannot give them everything they want in life.

Children who are not securely attached in early childhood have effectively suffered a trauma. In their adult lives, this trauma will most likely play out in problematic behavior around one or more of the basic human needs: trust (especially in relationships), self-care (especially managing emotions and impulses), food, sex (in romantic relationships), and money. I put "trust" first in that list because this quality is central for rising family leaders. Insecurely attached people struggle to trust others and to manage their own emotions effectively. A family enterprise leader with these kinds of flaws will create discord in the family circle, tending to be suspicious of others' motives and overly sensitive to criticism.

Forming a strong moral core

Second, we'll watch the child form a strong moral core, the foundation for knowing right from wrong, which will serve them for a lifetime. Different cultures have different standards of behavior and beliefs, but they are all taught the same way around the world: through stories and lessons learned in early childhood. For defense of right against wrong, and in pursuit of fulfilling lives, we teach virtues. Think of virtues as the muscles you train at the gym to protect your core. Strong moral core development from early childhood helps make kids financially and socially responsible for the rest of their lives.

Wealthy children are especially vulnerable to the erosion of their moral core. This is because wealth is a strong corrupting force that tends to work against virtues such as compassion and honesty. As parents and elders in the family enterprise, you should always be ready to show children that ethics transcend economics.

Parental engagement is imperative

A new baby is a blessing to every family. But it is parents, not extended family members, who have the primary responsibility for their children's moral development. In order to exercise that effectively, parents must be present and they must engage. Parents trying to grow their business may be so busy that they're not mindful of cultivating secure attachment. Yet attachment is not optional. Parents need their children to believe that they are the highest guarantor of the child's health and safety. This doesn't mean spending all day with your children. It does mean setting a high priority on the frequency, regularity, and focused attention you give your children. One or a few consistent rituals can make the bond secure: always having breakfast together, having an hour of play time daily, or being the one to read your child a bedtime story and settle them to sleep.

Don't blame yourself, stressed parents. But do be self-aware. Working in the family company, with its natural ups and downs, impacts your mood. Be aware of your mood swings and try not to let them have a negative impact on the secure attachment process for your child. If you're in a bad mood in front of your small child, explain to her that your bad mood is not because of her, so that your child does not feel responsible and somehow "bad" in her parent's eyes.

Parents are not, however, the only drivers of their child's moral development. From the time that a toddler is placed in a childcare setting or starts school, other people—household members, nannies, teachers, religious leaders, camp counselors—will be engaged in their moral development. For enterprising families, crafting these influences is particularly important. Keep it simple; what you need to insure is that your small child is learning the difference between right and wrong, getting the reinforcement that is appropriate to their age and stage of development, and consistently developing "muscles" (virtues) to support that moral core. Ask yourself: who are the people we want to influence our child? Can they teach lessons that will build our child's moral core? What can we do to ensure that these important relationships are benefiting our child?

It's only when a young child is equipped with the foundations of psychological health and a strong moral center that they're able to cultivate traits associated with effective leadership.

The "Rising Generation's Burden"

There is no such thing as "one child families" in family enterprise. Children growing up in a business family always have to contend with the "other child" at the table: that is, the company, office, or foundation that demands so much of their parents' attention. This dynamic raises an obstacle to building a solid foundation in emotional well-being. The primary attention of the whole family is on the business. At the dinner table, on vacation, whenever her parents aren't there—she can only feel that the absence is all for the "other child."

In addition, your child might rely too much on money to solve their problems. Healthy people don't pad their relationships with the protection of wealth. Instead, they build and manage relationships, in large part, with "the ties that bind"—bonds forged in struggle. Whether those struggles are shared or simply acknowledged and respected, it is clear that people prefer trusted connections with people who can help them face life's challenges.

As we've seen from the Grant and Glueck studies, fulfilling relationships are not optional; they are essential to happiness and emotional health. If wealth gets in the way, making it unnecessary for young people to struggle through conflicts and learn how to manage relationships effectively, they won't be able to establish and maintain long-term, fulfilling bonds as adults.

One next-generation member from a leading fifth-generation business family said to me when I was advising his family, The danger with wealth is that when you are in a conflict, whether it's a business or a personal situation, it will always seem very easy to just walk away. You say to yourself, "I don't need the relationship. I can always find others. And even if I can't, with my money I can always go it alone."[11]

Although that young man was making an astute observation, it is out-of-date. Today's collaborative economy makes it impossible, even for the wealthiest, "to go it alone." Relationships matter now more than at any other time in history. That's why it is particularly important for parents to pay attention to their children's significant affiliations. Honor and support those bonds. This gives the signal that important relationships are not disposable.

The issue of fair treatment is also important in family enterprise because money and privileged rights that are not merit-based are often associated with power and status within the family. For example, I often see that patriarchs prefer sons to become successors instead of daughters. This may be a result of outdated thinking, or perhaps they think that running an operating company is a major headache, and they don't want their daughter to be overburdened if she becomes occupied with raising her own children. It is gendered treatment nonetheless. Daughters who are career minded often tell me that they feel unfairly treated. They don't feel that they are seen as full members of the family enterprise with equal privileges and opportunities.

Waiting for the Marshmallows

As babies and infants grow into toddlers and small children, our vital job is helping them learn to care for themselves emotionally, building skills such as self-control and self-soothing. For parents, it takes a great deal of patience. For instance, when your child is having a tantrum, they are experiencing extreme emotions that they are ill-equipped to manage. It is the primary caregiver's job to patiently help the child manage those emotions constructively.

Today's children are bombarded by marketing messages that exploit children's impulsive behaviors and ingrain them ever more deeply. From the age of three onwards, it is vital for children to build healthy impulse control. To do this, they need to learn skills in delayed gratification. Adult caregivers must "be in the moment" with children when their impulsive desires are triggered, then calmly guide them toward delaying instant gratification. Usually this involves presenting children with attractive alternatives.

The most famous study of self-control in early childhood is known as "the marshmallow test." Developed in the late 1960s by psychologist Walter Mischel, then a professor at Stanford University, this series of studies presented preschoolers with one marshmallow. The preschooler could eat the one tantalizing treat in front of them *now*, or they could wait three agonizingly long kid-minutes and have two treats. In the late 1980s, decades after testing the preschoolers on self-control, a follow-up study with those same participants showed a strong correlation between their willpower in early life and their capabilities as adults. Children who were more successful in resisting the immediate reward grew up to be adults who were similarly strong in willpower. A preschooler's capacity for self-regulation, it turns out, may last a lifetime.[12]

Adults in business families may be so fully occupied with their work, they don't have the headspace to reinforce delayed gratification behavior in their children. Often, parents will give in to the child's pestering for candy or a new toy so that they can get on with their work. A typical scenario in both Asian and Western business families involves the patriarch having a child late in life, in his fifties or later. He doesn't spend very much time with the youngster, so he makes a special effort for the child to like him. Presents, after all, are the best bribes. But adults, before you give into your own impulses, think of your child's higher needs rather than their immediate desires.

Work Ethic and the Growth Mindset

A related concept to delayed gratification is work ethic. The Grant Study also showed that work ethic is one of the most important predictors of adult mental health.[13] Those who learn early to choose something they love to do, work at it to overcome challenges, and finally achieve what they set out to do, will excel at working through adversity and experience fulfillment throughout their adult lives.

Dr. Carol Dweck, psychology professor at Stanford University, developed the concept of the growth mindset with her research team. After studying the behavior of thousands of children, Dr. Dweck coined the terms "fixed mindset" and "growth mindset" to describe the underlying beliefs people have about learning and intelligence. When students believe they can get smarter, they understand that effort makes them stronger. Therefore, they put in extra time and effort, and that leads to higher achievement.[14]

In summary, it's a good idea from an early age to instill discipline and hard work. Try to strike a balance when you help kids choose their enrichment activities. You don't want to throw them to the wolves, allowing social pressures and peer influencers to drive them toward activities you don't approve of, but you also don't want to dictate all their choices. Many kids engage in competitive sports. Others pursue music, debate, theater, dance, 4H, robotics camp, or even gaming, among countless enrichment offerings. These help create muscle memory of dogged determination and the sense of fulfillment when mastery is achieved—both so important in carrying the family torch.

My parents started me on piano when I was very young. Let's face it: it was hardly my choice at three and a half. Throughout my childhood I practiced studiously for a couple hours every day. I remember practicing and looking out the window, asking myself, "Why am I caged in this room while all the other kids are out playing?" Over time, piano practice not only gave me discipline, but joy. I grew to appreciate music in a way I would never have learned, had I not practiced so hard. Looking back, I now realize that music appreciation was a gift I gave myself. Even today, music anchors my life in the rough patches.

So, now I'm a mother. How do I approach the musical education of my own child? I decided to give my daughter music lessons only if she asked. To show my good faith, I started her on a couple months of lessons so she could get her feet wet. She didn't practice.

Instead of nagging her, I asked, "Do you want to continue? If you do, you need to practice. If not, we should stop." And so she moved on to other things. Years went by. Imagine my surprise when suddenly my daughter took up the piano on her own. She taught herself through YouTube! Some of my friends are reporting the same story of self-study among their own kids. I think this portends good things for their life skills, such as resilience and self-motivation for lifelong learning. Even more importantly for family enterprise, self-starting kids create structure in their lives and define their own success.

What Kind of Person Is Your Child?

Having a sense of your own identity means being able to recognize the unique qualities you possess as an individual, especially the positive attributes of which you can be proud. Even before a child reaches the age of ten, it is possible—and desirable—for them to recognize how those internal qualities help them to navigate the world around them. As they explore and navigate, they will develop proclivities as problem solvers. For example, some kids will be inclined to invention when solving a problem, others will be inclined to management or logistics. Parents should try to assess the range of identities and problem-solving tendencies early by setting up experiments. This can happen in the home, when kids are given real problems to solve. Or it can happen on the road, when parents (usually traveling alone with one child), leave problems for the child to solve. Don't over schedule your kids with managed activities!

If "identity" seems too mature a concept for a child to be aware of, consider these examples. A well-organized, self-motivated child knows how to plan and get things done on time and often is looked up to by her peers. A very social child is good at relationships, can "read a room," and often proves persuasive. An impulsive child with good self-control (able to withstand the allure of marshmallows!) can make timely decisions. A compassionate child can ease tension during conflict; a highly verbal child with empathy can mediate a conflict. Daily outcomes at home, on the playing field or at the playground give attentive parents the chance to reinforce awareness in their young child about what positive qualities led to the good outcomes. For example, you might notice that your child solved a problem. You can lightly reinforce your child's identity by saying, "You fixed it. How did you do that?" The child may or may not be able to answer. But you should follow up with the facts, such as: "I saw you watching closely. You are observant."

Developing one's own unique identity, apart from wealth and apart from the family company, is especially difficult for a child in a business family. If yours is a family of overachievers, that can make it even harder for a child to measure up. Difficult though it may be, creating one's own identity is especially important in the family business context. For a child, this is what will make him feel unique and valuable. He will nurture that identity, taking pleasure at excelling at the things he sees that he is good at. From this identity will spring his confidence and self-esteem. Your child will be comfortable in his own skin.

Western cultures give more scope for young people to define their identities in a way that fits their unique self while being considered positive by their community. By comparison, Asian cultures have more rigid standards of defining identities that are considered positive. For example, because of the Confucian teaching of filial piety, being a good rising leader means shouldering your parents' burdens, which translates to taking over the operating companies. So, being a successful entrepreneur might not be seen as being a responsible steward, especially if there is only one rising leader. Conflicts sometimes arise across generations because of these rigid definitions and limited options, since there are still relatively few well-accepted, positive identities from which rising leaders can choose. I encourage Asian family business leaders to support all worthy endeavors that rising leaders take on, whether inside or outside the family company.

Early Childhood Is the Perfect Time to Learn Core Values

Core values are the fundamental beliefs held by a person or an organization—guiding principles that dictate behavior. Core values are what we use to help children understand the difference between right and wrong.

Consider a child's fascination with fire. The first time she's at risk of getting burned, her senses make her pull back. Her senses teach her that fire is dangerous—and powerful. So what stops her from pushing her baby brother into the fireplace in anger? Only the awareness that it is wrong. To make the connection, we need to explain that it is wrong to harm living things. When we impart this understanding, we're teaching core values.

Families with religious affiliations might draw on those foundations for their core values. In the West, that may mean turning to Bible stories; for Asian families, it may involve Confucian teachings. (And of course, the array of religious traditions extends far beyond just those two.)

These are good foundations. But it is important to add your family's unique core values. Aside from universal values (such as love and empathy), I've seen core values differ from family to family. Some emphasize work ethic or philanthropy, others focus on independence, risk taking and entrepreneurship. Whatever they may be for your family, these shared values should be actionable ones that dictate behavior to bind the group together and foster unity. So, think through your family's core values, articulate them clearly, pass them down through stories, and be good role models through action.

But how to handle bad behavior? It's true, even core values can drive problematic behavior in children and adults. When values-based actions are taken to extremes, it can be like too much of a good thing. Accomplishments can come at the expense of a different core value. Let's look at risk taking as an example. In *Touching the Void*,[15] a harrowing story of survival, world class mountaineer Joe Simpson relates how his insatiable appetite for risk continually put his climbing partners in danger. In a 2011 interview with *The Telegraph*, Simpson admitted, "I'm not an easy person to be with."[16]

Parenting involves dealing with all kinds of problematic behaviors—from social aggression like bullying, to ethics lapses like cheating, to self-harm and substance abuse. Those things are beyond the scope of this book, but I encourage you to seek additional resources and further discussions as your needs arise.

The meaning and practice of core values need to be updated with the times. For example, frugality is often stated as a core value of business families. To demonstrate frugality, you have to save your money—not deploy it carelessly. However, as the family grows in wealth, overly frugal families often fall into the trap of being "penny wise, pound foolish." They may not be able to see the need to invest in a bigger footprint for the organization in order to professionalize and set the stage for the next growth phase.

Core values that are shared in your family need to be instilled with intentionality at an early age. Then when the time for succession comes, parents will feel that the family organizations they nurtured will be in good hands, because their own values are aligned with those of the incoming leaders. This activity can be coordinated by the family enterprise so that everyone in the next generation can take in the lessons at the same time, while strengthening their own peer relationships.

Conclusion

From birth to age ten, children benefit from the gifts you bestow on them. Not bicycles or train sets, but gifts of security, identity, core values, a growth mindset, and a healthy relationship with money. The child with good psychological and emotional health will demonstrate self-confidence and self-control, along with a clear understanding of right and wrong, and be free from an undesirable sense of entitlement. Parents can raise happy and well-balanced children in an environment of wealth: they can do this by creating a development plan that promotes secure attachment in their child. In these first ten years, parents can put in place the foundations for their emerging leaders to be the ones that tomorrow's world needs: able to self-regulate and steward social resources, stabilized by a strong moral core.

CHAPTER 6

Be Trustable to Teens

Teens have rich social networks, but they still need you to engage.

That moment in every parent's life: when you wake up and find a stranger in your house?

In place of the child who has always depended on you and looked to you for guidance is now a teenager bent on asserting their own identity and kicking against the constraints of your authority. Welcome to parenting teenagers!

Startling and exasperating though this stage of life may be for parents (and children too), it comes with unique rewards. Your child is finding his or her own place in the world, and you still get to participate in that. Indeed, you *must* participate: teenagers need more support than they may care to admit. On top of their already confusing lives, the teen children in family enterprises face additional complexities—such as awareness that their family's reputation may impact how others view them, and vice versa.

The good news is that as their parent, you can support your teen to develop their true sense of self, learn financial responsibility, become interested in the family enterprise, and learn how it can help support them. Start centerprising early!

During these years, your rising generation family members are growing in independence and freedom. This is the stage when they are first challenged intellectually and socially. In many societies, especially in Jewish families around the world, they will be required to take on adult responsibilities and navigate rites of passage. In other societies, as in China and the UK, they will either select (or be selected into) an academic track for life based on standardized test results. They might take an after-school job to earn spending money, learn to drive, embark alone on travel, and/or explore their newfound sexual maturity. They will definitely be more influenced by what their friends think than any opinion their parents may hold.

Teens often have polarized reactions to the family enterprise. Some rebel against all that it represents; others embrace it in admiration of their parents' accomplishments and/or the privileged lifestyle it brings. While parents cannot dictate teenagers' attitude and engagement with the family enterprise, you have a lot more influence than you think.

The teenage years can be a dangerous time. Adolescents make mistakes and judgment errors owing to the inexperience of youth, and some can have lasting consequences. They may experience new traumas and common maladies, from mild to serious, that require more self-care. And they may face life threatening perils: depending on the country and culture in which they are raised, those may range from epidemic levels of substance abuse, to highway deaths that affect teens more than any other group, to sexually transmitted infections, to acute or chronic travel-related illnesses.[1]

Some problems, especially certain health issues or run-ins with the law, are not fixable, no matter what resources you have at your disposal. For example, dispiriting studies now seem to indicate that dependency on heroin and other opioids causes changes in the brain that are not easily reversed.[2] Chronic addiction, if not fatal, will render your teenager a lifelong dependent whose special needs will drain the family enterprise financially and emotionally, becoming a major source of family conflict.

Wherever teens go, their inner world goes with them. Screen time opens them to the global world, and many teens are now working within the circles of their social networks to respond to threats and engage in positive change. In 2018, teens grappled with managing flop accounts on Instagram to ensure their trustability so they could have honest debates over issues of the day.[3] In 2019, teenagers spammed Instagram to fight back against child pornography.[4]

At the same time, teens report unique anxieties and concerns. They may become political, and their judgments can be harsh. Teenagers detest inconsistency and hypocrisy, especially from adults who they think should know (and behave) better.[5] Parents, teachers, coaches, and community leaders who show consistency in their own goals, values, and behavior will gain their respect.

Thankfully, for the rest of us, teenagers can be very, very funny. They are open to profound transformation. Teenagers are, for the most part, social animals. They are highly aware of their surroundings. They are the consumers to whom the world markets its goods and services for high growth. If you are seeking new sectors to grow your business, look no farther than the tastes and habits of your teenager. I know one family in the retail business where the matriarch regularly took her teenage daughter shopping just to observe her habits, to better inform the family company's strategy. During these outings, mother and daughter would naturally talk about business in free-flowing conversations. It gave the daughter opportunities to offer her mother creative suggestions about new products or improvements to consider for the family company. It was an empowering experience for the daughter. Over time, she felt ownership in the company and engaged proactively. Weighing in on family business became a welcome responsibility for her, rather than an unpleasant burden.

Heading off Trouble at the Pass

Taking an active part in your teenager's life and helping them find their passions, their trusted circle of friends and mentors, and a sense of comfort in expressing their true selves will require a high level of energy, attention, and conscious commitment. But it is important to get this right. During this confusing time, young people can easily go off the rails, getting into trouble in numerous ways. For a family enterprise, the costs of getting it wrong are extremely high. Short-term, it can create anxiety within the nuclear family and the wider family enterprise system. This takes the parents' attention away from building their business, and in the longer term it can lead to the loss of future talent for the family enterprise in the rising generation.

Parents are well advised to take a proactive approach, getting in front of these potentially problematic teenage situations to prevent them, rather than having to deal with trouble once it is already on your doorstep. Being reactive takes at least as much effort as being proactive, often with far less success.

Parenting your teenager effectively requires new learning and adaptation. To develop an authoritative voice that can influence your teenager, you need to gain their respect. You need to be trustable. That means showing authenticity in living your own life so you can be a good role model. Take time to learn their language—for instance, all the different "hacks" they're into (e.g., digital hack, life hack, etc.)—and try to remember that their world is heavily focused on experiential connections, which means "there's no words" for a lot of what they talk about. If you have built a family ecosphere, gear in with your teenager. That means taking a proactive stance in being an engaged part of their life, helping them build a trusted friendship circle, keeping abreast of their highs and lows—and showing up. The section below explores these strategies in more detail.

Concrete Strategies for Proactive Parenting

Spend time with your teen

Set up structures and routines that enable you to talk with them regularly one-on-one, in a context that encourages them to engage. Driving kids to their activities is an excellent example: you are in a quiet, self-contained space, sitting side by side but not face to face, which can be too confrontational for teens. These moments are harder to come by for urban families. Try walking the dog together, or doing the shopping—and turn your smartphone off! The odds are zero that your teen will turn hers off, but she is watching you. Model consistency in making time to focus on her without distractions—but act casual! A friend recently told me a funny story about this. After spending the afternoon with his teenage daughter (his only child), they met up by chance with Mom.

"Where have you been!?" Mom scolded Dad. "I've been calling you for hours!"

Dad reached into his pocket, took out his smartphone, and switched it back on.

"Dad!" said the teenager, rolling her eyes, "that is so irresponsible! Never turn your phone off! What if your child was trying to reach you!?"

Simple household chores like chopping vegetables or putting away dishes, or a regular evening stroll, offer a similar opportunity for conversation. If you can chaperone a group of teens on an evening out or to an extracurricular activity, there is the added bonus of being the "invisible observer," quietly listening to what your child's peer group talks about and how they interact.

Help your teen build a trusted friendship circle

During this age, young people need other healthy, key influencers who are not their parents. That excludes other elders in the family enterprise, too. Naturally, their friends will largely fill that role, so talk with them about what makes for a good friend. Sound casually knowledgable when you mention qualities such as loyalty and kindness. Use current events, the media, or even gossip to alert them to the warning signs of unhealthy relationships. This will equip your teen to make good choices. If the parent-child relationship is healthy, the child will generally listen to the adult's suggestions. If the parent, however, rejects all key relationships their child shows a liking for, the child will almost certainly reject the parent. The key is not to rebuff all of the teen's thinking about relationships. Validate their relationship premise, build on it, shape it, and guide your teen toward a reliable, healthy, trusted circle. You'll have a greater chance of success if you support some of your child's relationships, perhaps offering nuanced commentary on aspects of life where your child might rely on their friend's opinions and where they might find better advisors, while guiding them away from any outright bad influences, clearly explaining your reasoning to your teen.

Be on the lookout for strong resistance from your child when you recommend that they move away from certain relationships. That friendship may look sketchy on the outside and thus seem undesirable to you, but you may be missing a clue on the inside—some aspect of your teen's emerging identity that the relationship is serving (even if serving badly). If a child thinks he might be gay, for instance, he might gravitate toward gay friends and challenge cultural norms to explore that affinity. You have a decision to make about how you want to handle that, but the first step of the process is being aware. Unless you set out to achieve that kind of emotional sensitivity as a parent, you will never have even a hint of what your child is thinking and feeling.

Show up

Parents should make a point of showing up at their teens' performances and games. Your child may not say that it is important to them; they may even roll their eyes and seem exasperated. But having a parent who is simply *there*, who can be trusted to turn up, matters more than a teen may care to admit.

Show up on a more subtle level, too. If your teen has a curfew, make sure you are home when they get home. If they have household chores, you should have household chores too. Do yours loudly! Modeling good behavior will have a lasting impact on your teen. It's these small forms of engagement that give a young person the assurance that a caring, engaged adult does indeed notice where they are and what they are doing.

Teens Must Choose a Tribe

As a young person looks outside their family unit to understand themselves more fully, they will be wondering to which tribe they belong to. Are they the jock or the gamer? The rebel or the fashionista? Do they even have to be just one thing? If a boy feels, for example, that he's both jock and gamer, that combination of identities may not be accepted by his classmates. It will be necessary for him to work through exactly how important it is for him to be authentic to both of these identities, and whether he can wear them both comfortably within his chosen group of friends. Maybe he needs to cultivate a new group of friends with whom he can truly be himself. When was the last time you had to jettison your entire social network? Being a teenager can be really tough, and we often don't give teens the credit they deserve for courage and grit.

Coming from a business family, a young person can easily feel that they don't have true freedom in making decisions about their own life. Others may make quick assumptions and judge them. Sometimes, your kids may have to work even harder than their peers to define themselves, and they will need confidence and a higher level of maturity to assert their identity. Courage is needed, too, if their identity is not aligned with the norms within the family's own culture—a budding musician in a family whose wealth was made in retail, say. Let's hear it for Adam Levine!

The more passions that individuals uniquely possess within a family group, the more resources the family enterprise has for a Phoenix rising through a successful generational transformation and renewal. To recognize this rich family legacy takes wise elders. If that's the kind of wisdom you aspire to, your work will be to inspire each youth to perform beyond their individual best, to work together effectively with their siblings or cousins, and to contribute the fruits of their success to the family enterprise. All of this takes years to achieve. It should be planned and rolled out systematically starting when the family youngsters are sprouting. Cultivating the entire talent pool into future family leaders in areas of their choosing (with some guidance and encouragement of family elders as to the direction) is a decades-long process.

Building a Circle of Trusted Advisors

In the eyes of a teenager, their friends may be the ultimate authority on all things, but other people can and should start to play an important role. Engage other trusted people to play a part in your teen's life. By being proactively involved in guiding your child to build a trusted circle of advisors, parents can empower specific relationships. Perhaps a godmother can give wise advice without the burden of the parent-child relationship, or a twenty-something cousin can share their own recent experiences of traversing adolescence within the complications of a business family. Parents may also voice support for specific mentoring friendships where they see them as a force for good in the teen's life.

By bringing an array of relationships to your teen, you will effectively be guiding them to discern and understand for themselves what specific type of counsel they can get from each trusted voice. For example, a volleyball coach may be an excellent sounding board for feelings about being an inadequate athlete, or concerns about your teen's competitive nature (or lack of it), but probably not as well equipped to give counsel on the academic pressures of gaining admissions into top universities. Encouraging mentors from outside the family is a powerful way for parents to introduce young people to these kinds of relationship boundaries and help them to "use" these trusted circle resources effectively in their own development.

Being able to build a trusted circle of advisors is an important skill for rising family leaders who will likely live in a fish bowl as adults. It helps them (1) navigate complex human networks and relationship boundaries, (2) engage truth tellers who will mostly give them the good, the bad, and the ugly (not necessarily out of personal loyalty, but from moral convictions about right and wrong), and (3) distinguish between impartial views, self-interested views, culturally-colored views, and all the shades of gray in between.

Keeping it Real with Your Teen

In the previous chapter, we discussed how important it is to establish core values beginning in your child's first years of life. With those basic values set, the stage from eleven to twenty is the time to solidify your child's sense of their family identity. Help them to understand the history of the family, embrace its values, take pride in being a part of it, and feel a desire to contribute to it.

Do not assume that your child is naturally inclined to take pride in the the business family. They may not even have positive feelings toward it, let alone display them. Now that they're becoming more acutely aware of their family's social status and wealth, teens will have an array of different responses to their background. I have seen a range of reactions including pride, superiority, inadequacy, embarrassment, and guilt.

Unpleasant, painful, or embarrassing narratives can affect how warmly a teenager feels toward their own family. Examples might include:

- *Parents' divorce*: painful already, even in a private setting, but worse if it is in the public eye covered by the media.

- *Family fights*, especially over money and control of family assets, that create worry and stress as well as embarrassment if the fight is public.

- *Family secrets*, such as illegitimate children (becoming more common as genetic testing becomes cheaper and more popular), which can create instability and tension.

If such events occur, it is critical to have active ongoing discussions with your teens about what is happening and what the aftermath means for them and for the family as a whole. Clear communication is key here. Do not talk down to your teen. Whether public or private, scandals are adult matters that intrude on their adolescent lives. Do them the courtesy of treating them like an adult with the facts, because they may be expected to respond in the adult sphere. It's your job to prepare them for that. And remember, your teen is human, just like the rest of us. When they say they "don't want to talk about it," give them slack. Family problems aren't their fault.

That said, family elders should proactively cultivate a healthy sense of responsibility toward the family enterprise when the rising generation member is in their teens or early twenties. As a baseline, you are working toward them becoming:

- *Good, supportive owners*, ones who would be willing to sacrifice by foregoing distributions and perhaps even to contribute capital during tough times;

- *Guardians of the family's reputation* who avoid creating scandals;

- And hopefully, *active contributors* to the family enterprise with the Four Capitals at their disposal.

Having the Money Talk with Your Teens

One of the most important life skills a teenager can acquire is personal financial responsibility. The first step in acquiring this skill, along with the independence to exercise it, is setting clear expectations for both the present and the future. You as the parent have a role to play here.

Healthy financial habits can be ingrained early. The teen years are the best period to build the discipline that will later enable young people to pay their bills, file taxes, live within their means without excess personal debt, and protect their credit history.

Rather than handing your teenager a credit card and setting them free to spend whatever they want, it is wise to ask them to come up with a budget, then give guidance. If, for example, they have set aside a large chunk of their budget to buy expensive presents for their friends, you can take the opportunity to suggest a less money-oriented approach to their friendships. These conversations can, however, be minefields for tone deaf parents. You need to learn how to talk to your teen using their language. Irony, for example, is a popular tool for teenagers. It's one that you might try adopting to lighten up sensitive conversations.

In discussing your teen's budget, be clear about what parts of their spending you will and will not support. "Needs, not wants" is a good, go-to mantra that explains your financial responsibility as a parent. It's an expression teenagers understand and accept, just as securely attached children accept your authority when it comes to health and safety.

Say your teenager wants to buy expensive electronic devices. You might decide (and hopefully agree) that he needs to find a way to fund that habit. Give them good opportunities to earn money for their discretionary spending—perhaps by working for the family business.

Help your teenagers to figure out their financial goals and find ways to work toward them. When children have after-school commitments that prevent them from working for pocket money, once again you can turn to a modified form of "needs, not wants," where parents can agree to do their best to satisfy needs, as proposed and effectively argued by the teenager. But they reserve the right not to satisfy asks that fall in the "wants" column.

A healthy relationship with money can be hard to achieve. Financial capital is the easiest to value, so money can easily become the measure of everything, even those things we know money cannot buy.

By its nature, money is a key source of power that can be used to control behavior in other family members. It is important for seniors to avoid this use of power. To nurture love and empathy, elders need to practice financial discipline in their roles. When making a gift of money, there should be no strings attached. Practice consistency in treating all family members the same, with a transparent policy and implementation process. Fail, and you risk undermining the fairness principle that is a bedrock governance tool for enterprising families worlwide.

Striking a balance between money deprivation and money saturation isn't easy for most parents. What I see most often is that parents tend to swing between two extremes. Some parents, seeing money as the enemy of virtue, withhold material goods to such an extent that children become envious of their peers' material goods and obsess over material consumption. Other parents, seeing money as a good thing to be shared indiscriminately in the family, are much more indulgent than the parents of their children's peers. As a result, those children become the object of envy.

My advice is not to view money as good or bad. Instead, consider money as a powerful resource that can realize opportunities and make dreams possible in any area of choice. Celebrating examples of people using money cleverly or wisely at the right time, and demonstrating the same skill in your own actions, gives children the sense of the positive power that money can bring.

Intentional consumption is an important concept for young children to learn. Consumption is natural. It should not be denied across the board. The bestselling book, *Eat This, Not That!* by David Zinczenko and Matt Goulding, became a media franchise for a good reason.[6] The simplicity of the mantra teaches so many life skills at once: intentional and meaningful consumption, taking pleasure in food, lifelong education, and impulse control—along with a healthy sense of humor. You could extrapolate this model by teaching your kids, "Spend on this, not on that!" Wealth is a pleasure to use. Denial is unhealthy if you are punishing yourself for being part of a wealthy family. What is important is to develop real enjoyment in what you consume, along with the habit and skill of taking healthy pleasures.

These kinds of financial conversations help young people to clarify and decide what matters to them, and through that to define their own values.

Financial comfort has its trade-offs. Show teenagers what it means to set the right expectations. If they prefer to work at something that doesn't make money, or to enjoy their lives without working that hard, they may need to have expectations of a middle-class lifestyle. Articulate the type of lifestyle the family enterprise can help support. Many hardworking family business leaders are willing to support a minimum to middle-class lifestyle, but not more than that. Anything beyond that will have to depend on an individual's ability to generate their own wealth.

A word about teenagers and philanthropy. Your philanthropic traditions help develop core values for your family enterprise or ecosphere. But teenagers today are rapidly adapting this part of your DNA. Whereas in your generation, and that of your parents, charity was kept separate from business, doing good in the 21st century increasingly happens in the workplace, as part of the everyday lives of milennials and post-millennials. Even though many countries still do not offer financial incentives for social enterprise, many products by social entrepreneurs have gone global. Your teens know those brands, like Tom's shoes. In order to support teenagers who are passionate about doing good while doing good business, you may need to accept that they may have little interest in traditional philanthropy. Keep an open mind and stay flexible to support their involvement in doing social good.

Young people should know how they can expect their family to support them in the future, and what their own responsibilities will be in terms of earning their own living and taking care of their own financial lives. Parents can help teenagers think through the type of future lifestyle that they feel comfortable with and plan toward that.

It may be the case that the parents' lifestyle is not the same as the one the youth has or that the parents expect the youth to have. That can unintentionally send a confusing message to a teenager. This can go either of two ways:

First, parents tell their teenage children that they must be thrifty and prudent with their spending, yet the teens see their parents taking first-class flights, going to the most expensive restaurants, and buying designer-label clothing. The parents may need to explain to their children that they are at a different stage in their lives; for decades they worked hard at building their company. Now that they have achieved financial success, they are ready to enjoy the fruits of their labor. But their children are still in the phase of life where they need to be hungry to build their own successes. Spendy seniors should be careful with this narrative to justify frugality in your teens. Never be untruthful about your financial resources in ages past. The internet allows teenagers to price historical goods and services and to calculate historical wealth in today's dollars. And just as beauty is in the eyes of the beholder, family photo albums tell the truth that you may not want your teenagers to hear.

Second, children see their parents being unnecessarily thrifty, given the wealth that they have amassed. Warren Buffett, born in 1930, is a famous example of a frugal billionaire. One of the world's wealthiest men, he regularly buys his breakfast at McDonald's and still lives in the same home he bought in 1958 for $31,500.[7] Here, parents may explain why they choose to be thrifty. It may be a conscious discipline, a habit, or a life philosophy. For seniors taking this tack, there are fewer red flags. Just be aware that parsimony is not the virtue to the "do good" generation as it was to the Silent Generation. Out of step with his generation, Warren Buffett pledged in 2010 to give away 99% of his wealth upon his death.[8]

At both ends of the spectrum, it is important for parents to explain to their children why there is a discrepancy between their expectations of their children, the level of family wealth, and their own spending habits. The explanation will most likely be different for every family, but the key is to have open dialog about it.

Be clear about your family's financial policy toward its members and strive for a level playing field. When parents don't support all of their children based on the same financial standard, teenagers in particular can easily read that as a sign that parents love one child more than another. In reality, it may be that one child is better at sweet-talking the parents (or hassling them!), or maybe it is the parent's mood in any given moment that induces them to buy one child a car and not do the same for the other child. Over time, children may build up a picture that they have been treated unfairly.

Too much of this in the family enterprise will, once again, poison the wellspring of the sacrosanct fairness principle.

What Does "The Best School" Really Mean?

Parents often ask me if it is important to send their teenagers to the best schools and whether they should push them to achieve good grades. Sending them to a school with the highest academic standards sometimes means a teen must live apart from their family. Generally, my advice is that healthy interaction with parents and siblings is more important for the rising generation than attending the "best" school. Parents guide values, cultivate confidence, and instill a sense of identity within the family enterprise, while sibling interaction makes for family unity in the future.

Many Chinese, African, Indian and Middle Eastern parents opt to send their children outside the country to receive Western style education. If you do decide to send your children abroad for high school, try to send all siblings to the same city or at least to the same country. Don't send one to the U.S. and another to Australia, because the learned cultural differences might impede long-term relationships among siblings.

Choosing the right school means selecting an institution that fits your child's learning style, where they can be at their best and develop confidence and a competitive spirit, and through rigorous standards gain the satisfaction derived from meeting high expectations. Grades are not the only measure of achievement. I encourage parents to help their teens understand that there are many paths to success. The family enterprise should reinforce this by centerprising. This approach supports an entrepreneurial spirit of flexibility and gives your child the adaptability they require to become effective rising family leaders.

If your teenager is not academically talented, refrain from pushing them to fit into that particular box. This is especially difficult in Asia where academic performance, future financial prospects, and social standing are all bound together. Elders need to remember that their future family leaders are likely to be the ones to set standards and competitive guideposts, not necessarily to follow them. That spirit is what will lead the Phoenix to rise. Therefore, it is important to empower them to define and even create their own framework, excelling at their chosen field either ahead of their competitors or bettering their own game if they are already ahead. Spend time helping them to build their framework. At the same time, let them know that there are still standards and expectations. Drifting and idling should never be their endgame.

Stoking the Fires in Passionate Teens

If your teenager is clearly talented and ambitious, all of the principles given above apply, along with some additional considerations. For the truly creative, competitive, talented, and driven rising generation members, try to cultivate their wealth creation abilities together with their passion.

The traits associated with effective leadership can mostly be developed at this stage, over and above any predisposition your teen may possess. They include:

- *Qualities associated with high performance*: persistence and grit; the ability to listen to others, incorporate their opinions, and make decisions; the ability to inspire a group and mobilize them; and courage, demonstrating bold but calculated risk taking.

- *Resilience*: experience with overcoming difficulty and learning from failure; an awareness that "bad stuff happens" in life; acceptance of setbacks in the normal course of events; plus the ability to tolerate failure when it happens and cope with the consequences.

- *A productive outlook on achieving goals*: believing that any goal is possible. An optimistic or pessimistic outlook tends to be a stable trait, conferred at birth, but a leader needs to be willing to aim for stretch goals, and able to achieve them.

- *Curiosity and creative problem-solving*. Especially valuable are people who try to link ideas from different fields, and do not give up in trying to find solutions, together with those who persist in seeking solutions that require seeing a problem from different perspectives, and then deciding on the best course.

- *The ability to deal with uncertainty* and decide on the best among a bad set of options, to stay steady until you see the positive or negative impact of your course of action, and then to make adjustments, if necessary.

- *Self-awareness*: to know your impact on others, seeing when you are right and admitting when you are wrong—then changing course.

Observe your teenager's temperament and behavior to see what type of wealth creation they gravitate toward. We will discuss this in detail in the next chapter. But in brief, the three main types are intrapreneurs (who thrive within an existing organization and seek to improve it from within), entrepreneurs (who create a compelling, new identity through the culture of a new venture), and portfolio builders (who set out to gather investments with strategic value). Of these three, there is a particular need for parents to help teenagers figure out if they have the capacity to be entrepreneurs. I deliberately say *capacity* here: while some aspects of entrepreneurship may be innate or else can be taught, the entrepreneurial wealth creator requires a particularly strong conviction to pursue their goals. Ask these questions:

1. Is this person willing and able to tolerate financial pain, sacrifice stability, and have the deep confidence to be a contrarian?

2. Do they have the courage to keep moving forward despite strong resistance?

3. Are they stubborn, or are they open to suggestions, and willing to adapt or change? (There is a difference between listening to others' ideas and having the flexibility of mind to change direction when things don't work out, as opposed to changing course too easily and not listening to one's own conviction—or at the other extreme, being too rigid to change directions when things haven't worked out over a long time.)

These qualities may be hard for parents to discern in their own children. If you need to, seek out the opinion of a trusted advisor, whether a relative or someone outside the family, who has observed your adolescent over a period of time and in different circumstances.

Entrepreneurship can be encouraged and assessed at the same time. For example, if a teenager is a cyclist and wants to spend the summer on a cycling trip, their parent may shut the plan down by saying, "No, that's a waste of time." Or they can nudge their child toward a more entrepreneurial approach by saying, "That's a good idea, but you have to fund it yourself." Brainstorm about ways they can get sponsorships, perhaps from travel companies or bicycle manufacturers. Then stand back and see whether your child is willing to execute.

Conclusion

Being a parent to teenagers is by nature a challenging exercise. Add the layer of complexity that exists within a business family, and it can seem utterly overwhelming. But stick with it. The outcomes can be deeply satisfying, as indeed the process can be as you develop a rich relationship with your teenager, the rising leader.

CHAPTER 7

Fast Tracking Your Almost Phoenixes

Engage your rising wealth creators now, or lose them forever.

Not too long ago, incubators were only found on farms and in hospitals. On the farm, incubators provided a safe place for eggs to hatch. Eventually, a baby chicken pecked its way out of the shell and into the world. In hospitals, incubators nurtured babies, especially sick or premature ones, providing them with the stable conditions they needed to survive the first hours of life. Today, an incubator is a place to cultivate the latest crop of twenty-something entrepreneurs. A safe place for the experimentation that leads to breakthroughs, incubators provide the ideal environment for new companies to take shape and startup companies to thrive. They're also proving grounds where entrepreneurs demonstrate their capacity for wealth creation. Take a stroll through any business incubator or accelerator, and you'll see that it's a tough and intensely competitive environment.

Being twenty-something is far from easy. We know, from the Grant Study, that for young men, their fathers will play a central role, whether in a positive or negative fashion. So patriarchs, be thoughtful, sensitive, engaged, and intentional about guiding your rising generation's career paths while they are in their twenties. The complexity of family enterprise and ecosphere means that they need guidance. If this feels too awkward for you, ask an external advisor to help. That was the move that catapulted transformation and growth at Arezzo, remember? Don't miss this critical period to help a rising leader investigate his unique identity in relation to the family enterprise. You only get a short time together to explore whether he can gear into the family enterprise.

Encouraging a twenty-something's interest in the family business requires careful planning. Take the case of the talented son of an industrial family who began his career at a financial services company outside of his family business upon college graduation. After a few years, when the young man had some experience under his belt, his father asked him to come work for the family's industrial distribution business. The son agreed. His father assigned the President of the company to supervise him, but there was no thoughtful career plan in place. The son was sent to another city, far from his family, to manage distribution for a geographic area. One of his assignments was to oversee the warehouse. With no clear learning objectives, assigned to what he perceived as low-level responsibilities, the young man quickly became frustrated and resigned within months. It was a tragically wasted opportunity to draw this accomplished twenty-something into the family business: his talent was lost to them all because of a badly planned talent development program.[1]

Young Adults Want Independence—But Engagement Too

For the first five to ten years after a young adult graduates from college or graduate school, the world is their oyster. There's a sense of freedom from the constraints of mandatory education and the strictures of parents. And most young adults are not yet tied down with a permanent relationship or children. This is the time for them to explore their identities, both independently and in relation to the family enterprise, figuring out what they want to do with their lives, where they want to settle down, what type of work they like, and who will be their partner in a long-term relationship.

While this young adult works through these decisions, it is valuable for the patriarch or matriarch of the family enterprise (and/or the parents, if they are not the same people) to be in close, regular dialog with them. Their job is mainly to provide opportunities and act as a sounding board, making it clear that they'd like to find a suitable place for the young adult within an existing family organization or help her create a gear linked to the family enterprise. The best person for this job is usually the family leader. (Remember, the family leader may be the controlling owner or another person who may be playing a governance role and not even working in the core business.) Nobody else will do, because that person has the highest authority to engage the rising generation in official roles. This signals to the young family member that the family enterprise considers her career development a top priority.

Meanwhile, the rest of the family elders can spend this decade most productively by overseeing the development of every candidate in the family talent pool. Work with each of them to chart out their career paths. Brainstorm together about specific roles (both full- and part-time) and design their career trajectories together. Help them see their future career options in the family enterprise or linked in with the family ecosphere.

For most families, this exploration period is likely to last about a decade. It will be shorter for others, but regardless of the duration, what's important is to guide the career and life planning of the next generation and have active discussions with these twenty-somethings before they put permanent structures in their lives.

A ten-year study led by John Davis focused on the rising generation in business families. The findings show that, in general, young adults do not like elders to tell them what to do.[2] However, they sincerely appreciate advice and guidance—when they ask for it. They also appreciate being offered interesting opportunities that they can choose to explore. Keeping this in mind, it is wise for family elders to avoid giving unsolicited advice. Instead, if you see that the rising family talent is gravitating toward a path that might not be ideal, ask them probing questions. Help by presenting what-if scenarios. This helps them visualize the potential outcomes of their choices.

Three Types of Wealth Creators

When your next generation is in their twenties, it is the perfect time to test whether they have the capacity and the desire to be business Phoenixes entrusted with growing the financial wealth. There should ideally be at least one wealth creator (preferably more) in each generation. Failing that, the backup plan for every family enterprise is to develop readiness in a family leader competent enough to make the key business decisions in each generation.

Any singular business leader will always need to coordinate with the family ownership group so they can deploy the resources they need to act on business decisions and carrying out their plans to grow family wealth. Without this close coordination (involving decisions made by more than one person), there is no decisiveness for wealth creation in a family enterprise. And of course, it is also important to use force multipliers to develop other non-business Phoenixes who can deliver a quantum impact for the family enterprise.

There isn't just one type of wealth creator. There are three distinct types. John Davis and I formulated these three categories of wealth creators in the early 2010s, while we were conducting a family wealth study. We looked at thirty years of data from the Forbes 400 list of "America's Richest Families."[3] Examining the list from its inception in 1982 through 2012, our sample group contained only those families that made the list from the start. We tracked the characteristics of families that were able to keep growing their wealth. We studied the manner in which they achieved this growth and compared those traits and methods alongside those of families that experienced a decline in wealth. Finally, we were able to see clearly how the wealth decline came about. And more importantly, how the wealth creation happened. In the successful families, there had been at least one person in every generation who excelled at building wealth for the family. What surprised us was this: champion wealth creators are not all created alike!

Here are the three categories of wealth creators we identified.

Intrapreneur: they embrace and transform the existing organization, which is often the legacy family company.

Intrapreneurs thrive in existing organizations and seek to improve them from within. They are collaborative, reasonably good with processes, and adept at cultural transformations. A great example of an intrapreneur is Whitney MacMillan, fourth-generation leader of Cargill. During his ten-year tenure as CEO, MacMillan grew the business from $10 billion to $33 billion, diversifying its activities by exposing it to the consumer market and in the process securing its place as the world's largest grain company.[4]

Entrepreneur: they create a new organization that has a compelling business model and is propelled to success by its novel and unique identity and culture.

Entrepreneurs thrive outside organizations. They know how to spot market opportunities. They know how to deploy a small, agile, dedicated team to monetize the opportunity they seize. They are able to scale effectively. They are eloquent about the unique value of their new products or services. This combination—what they do or make, and how they show it off—creates a loyal following. Consider the example of David René de Rothschild who, with his cousin Eric de Rothschild, rebuilt Banque Rothschild (the Paris-based banking business, which was independent from the other financial services businesses owned by Rothschild family members) from scratch in 1982, after their existing bank was nationalized by the French government. As David famously told Francois Mitterand, "I used to be an inheritor, but now I am a founder."[5]

Portfolio Builder: they build wealth using financial assets and real property, not organizations.

Portfolio Builders are able to piece together capital investments with strategic value. They employ financial participation in emerging industries or technologies to create long-term, above average market returns. Jay Pritzker is an excellent example of a third-generation rising leader who, with his brother Robert, pieced together a group of manufacturing and services businesses, starting in 1953 with Colson Corporation, a struggling metal-goods manufacturer. Through six decades they built a mega-business called Marmon Holdings, valued at more than $7.7 billion in 2007. Alongside stakes in businesses ranging from airlines to casinos, the Pritzkers' best-known brand is the Hyatt hotel chain, which began in 1957 when Jay bought their first hotel for $2 million.[6]

The Mindset of Wealth Creators

Regardless of the type of wealth creator, they must have an innovative and entrepreneurial mindset. Compared with others in the family enterprise or ecosphere, they most closely resemble founders of tech startups in their attitude toward risk. Your wealth creators usually want to experiment often and make keep/kill decisions quickly. Their behavior may create dissonance in the family, and maybe even at work, but this is normal. They are, without a doubt, the best catalysts for innovation.

The innovative mindset adopts an attitude to problem-solving that addresses any specific difficulty in a game-changing way. Innovation can be learned. It is possible to learn how to become a creative, out-of-the-box problem solver through the many books, articles, and podcasts that are available on the subject. Many large family companies, such as Ford, employ coaches in creative thinking, and several universities now offer doctoral programs in creative studies.[7] So it's now possible to work with experienced advisors in this area.

The entrepreneurial mindset has three parts. The first is an "inclination to discover, evaluate, and exploit opportunities."[8] The second is an appetite for relentless pursuit of improvements until success is achieved. Many persistent people can be dogged, but the entrepreneur remains open-minded and flexible enough to reexamine assumptions as needed. Third is the tolerance of risk. No matter how much you analyze or plan, new ventures involve the unknown. At some point, the entrepreneurially-minded person needs to accept the unknown risk and take the plunge. Waiting until you can contain all of the risks means that entrepreneurship never happens. As LinkedIn co-founder Reid Hoffman says, entrepreneurship is like "throwing yourself off a cliff and assembling an airplane on the way down."[9]

Before you meet the wealth creators, let's talk about a practical issue in wealth creation—financial support. Senior leaders who have successfully prepared their wealth creators will have real talent on their hands with significant potential. You will have to support these projects financially. When Phoenixes go out to fundraise for their early projects, the first question they're going to hear is, "how much has your family put in?" Major sums will be involved. You probably have made many capital commitments as part of your current wealth management strategy. Don't let these commitments become a major obstacle for you, your family, and your rising leaders. Keep enough flexibility in your capital allocation. You'll need the dry powder.

Now that you've met the three kinds of wealth creators, you probably want to determine what kind you've got in your own family. To start with, let's take a look at profiles depicting each wealth creator in their natural habitat and on a promising career path.

Profile of an Intrapreneur

You will easily recognize the intrapreneur in your emerging-generation group by two characteristics. First, she thrives in leading and improving an existing organization and processes. She might have been class president in school, or captain of the hockey team. She probably works inside the existing operating company; if she is talented, she will eventually take over as CEO and/or chairman. For the intrapreneur, there are two broad career paths available.

The insider

This intrapreneur's first paid job is usually in the family company, and he works his way up through the ranks. Except for an internship or two during college (sometimes in relevant industries, or in related fields as a way to broaden their horizon and practice exploring), it is rare for this type of intrapreneur ever to have worked anywhere else. A great example is Bill Ford, who grew up in a loving family with two parents hailing from iconic family enterprises (Ford and Firestone), but without much support or direction from his uncle, then-CEO Henry Ford II.[10] After graduation, Bill plunged headlong into a heavy rotation of unglamorous, middle management jobs at Ford—many abroad or in the backwaters. Twenty years after leaving Princeton, Bill was leading Ford's heavy truck division. In 1999 he set aside his executive career to join the board of Ford Motor Company, anticipating his father's retirement after serving on the board for fifty years. Bill shelved his ambition, gave up the limelight, and set to work alongside his father. Two years later, as Ford struggled to stem losses, the directors fired CEO Jacques Nasser and asked Bill to lead the company as CEO. Bill Ford was elected Chairman of the board five years after. As Chairman, Bill steered the company through the crippling financial storm of 2008, expanded markets in China and India, and grew one of the world's most iconic brands, currently on Interbrand's ranking of the global top fifty.

Being an insider has its advantages. Growing up inside the business gives you intimate knowledge of the family company. You have the chance to build trust, confidence, and a strong track record, not only with the senior family leader, but also with the non-family management team. The value of this cannot be overestimated. Rising family leaders must be able to win the confidence of non-family senior management. While any rising CEO needs to build their own, younger, management team, they can't do that right away. It is a process that takes time, and the wisest, like Bill Ford, know how much they have to learn from the current management. For their part, managers will generally only be willing to groom next generation leaders if their own goals are aligned with their protégés' success. They must believe that their protégés are capable, and they must be secure and psychologically healthy enough to groom family intrapreneurs with goodwill. For this reason, it is of enormous importance for seniors to choose non-family managers carefully. And incentivize them appropriately.

There are many reasons why intrapreneurs may face limited career options if things don't go as hoped or planned inside the family company. They may be the losers when their vision clashes with that of the senior generation. Or when the young insider feels they are not given responsibility and decision authority fast enough. Or perhaps the senior leader won't retire and make way for the capable rising generation to lead. The senior leader may feel the rising generation is not good enough, or not yet ready, to take over as Chairman or CEO—yet they like having them involved in the company, so they delay making any formal succession plan. Eventually the young insider will feel frustrated and want to leave, but they will feel stuck because there are limited options outside the company equal to the rank and status available inside the family business. Rising family leaders usually do not share these thoughts with the senior family business leader. But these common concerns are at the top of their minds. Family elders and business leaders who want to attract younger family talent would achieve higher success keeping these considerations in mind.

The explorer

This intrapreneur is driven to prove herself outside the family sphere first, before joining the family enterprise. In so doing, they learn how other companies are run, providing a competitive benchmark for their family business. They bring valuable learning back into their own company, too, along with an array of high value skills, notably in investment banking or finance. Manufacturing businesses can use these skills and the social networks that come with them. They are useful when growing strategically, via mergers and acquisitions.

The explorer knows how healthy it is to gain support outside the "fish bowl" of their own family enterprise. They work hard to create an independent identity, which almost always builds the confidence of their team. They create options for themselves, together with the benefits of their own professional relationships and networks, mentors, and friends who give advice based on what is best for this individual, rather than what is best for the family enterprise.

The worldly explorer carries the spark of pioneering spirit and is rarely afraid to learn how other people do things to stay competitive and cutting-edge. The challenge, for the family, is luring them back into the family enterprise! If they're doing well in their profession in the outside world, what does the family enterprise have to offer? Axel Dumas made a very deliberate and strategic decision to work in banking initially, building a career with BNP Paribas before joining the family business, Hermès. His financial expertise proved to be critical when he became chief executive of Hermès in

2014, in the midst of LVMH's hostile takeover attempt. Under his leadership, the family rallied to maintain control of Hermès. "For us, speaking of families, it's important that the young generation who want to join have a successful career outside (the business)," says Dumas. "We need them to construct themselves, first."[11]

Whether insider or explorer, both types of intrapreneurs have great potential for success. The path you choose together will depend on their interests and available opportunities at the time.

Profile of an Entrepreneur

The entrepreneur wealth creator will always work best outside the business to create new value based on market opportunity. Watch for this budding talent as early as the grammar school years. Financier and environmentalist Ben Goldsmith, founder of WHEB, got in trouble for reselling golf balls from his country club at age nine.[12] You might see an uptick in activity during the teenage years. Shoe designer Alexandre Birman, founder of Schutz, turned an empty lot into a parking business and bought his first car with the profits. Your young entrepreneur might start by hacking their favorite products for custom use—then start taking orders. They turn ideas into realities. This is the family member who starts a company—most often, a new business—that sits entirely outside of the family's core businesses. Such talent is precious to your family, but it can be challenging to handle.

When the entrepreneur is just starting out and trying to get traction with a new idea, the rest of the family may well view them as a failure whose ideas are going nowhere. Imagine the impact this has, psychologically, on the entrepreneur. While they're in this start-up phase, the energy and hard work required, plus the daily unpredictability, goes beyond levels sustainable in any organization in your family enterprise. Again, imagine that. It is often difficult to do so—especially for multigenerational families that may have grown used to the steady pace exhibited by the existing businesses.

The entrepreneur's pace will be grueling, with a daily schedule more akin to that of a pro athlete than a business manager. Your entrepreneur is a high-performing, Type A individual. This can further isolate them. Encourage mutual understanding and appreciation during this delicate stage, knowing that high performers, like entrepreneurs, are not always easy to get along with. Once they do succeed, though, their status (measured by wealth, fame, and power) shoots up quickly in a short period of time. At that time, they likely will not want to be constrained by the family enterprise, with its complicated family dynamics. That's why, if you don't engage them before they succeed, you'll lose them forever.

I see many families pushing talented entrepreneurs away, simply because the family is not prepared for their success. The entrepreneurs are left without any motivation to contribute to the family enterprise. Put yourself in their shoes and ask yourself, "Why would I work so hard to create wealth for everyone else?" This is a natural question. It does not generally come from arrogance, nor does the question imply disrespect on the part of the entrepreneur for the family enterprise. Entrepreneurship is driven by taking a risk in anticipation of a reward, so naturally the entrepreneur in your family will apply that equation to their own efforts for the family enterprise.

The number one reason to evolve your family enterprise into an ecosphere is so that you can engage your entrepreneurs and not lose them. Centerprising will create a distributed system of innovation and entrepreneurship at the edge that can benefit the core. By centerprising, you can revive the founding pioneer spirit in the span of a single generation. Treat your entrepreneurs well, make them feel understood, stand by them through their false-starts, and they'll stick with you. If you don't do this, you'll never build the innovation culture you want.

For the Lee family, founders of Lee Kum Kee, entrepreneurial drive in the fourth generation took their 131-year-old legacy business in a fresh direction. Having built their wealth in producing sauces, the family survived a rift between third generation brothers, making unity more desirable, even critical, to their survival. Through the entrepreneurship of the youngest sibling, Sammy Lee, LKK Health Products Group Ltd was founded as a subsidiary of the legacy company in 1992, operating under the core brand Infinitus. Combining traditional Chinese medicine with modern insights into bioscience engineering, the business took off and then crashed in 1998 in the aftermath of the Asian financial crisis. Facing difficult choices about capital allocation, the family agreed after much debate to give Sammy five years to turn the business around. Their higher goal was to ensure that they would not be riven by another ownership split. In just four years, Sammy reached the company's five-year revenue goal. Today, both businesses—health products and sauces—are equally significant.[13]

Profile of a Portfolio Builder

The portfolio builder is outward-looking, somebody who builds wealth through investing. It may be harder to spot this budding talent in the family. Watch for quantifiable gains. If you've got a talented portfolio builder on your hands, gains will result when your teenager or young adult funds any project, usually by bringing two or more people (or assets) together and adding money. Be aware that early signs will probably involve more gains in social capital— like the young teen who invests "fan time" in emerging YouTubers or other influencers, then sees huge gains in their own social media accounts as a result. Eventually, the portfolio investor becomes obsessed with (and adept in) math and finance. They are skilled in betting on non-family entrepreneurs. They know how and when to make the right direct investments through co-investment networks with other families. They spot and sieze other attractive opportunities, especially those for seed-funding fast growing new industries. Learning the ropes along the way will later enable the portfolio builder to increase the invested capital.

What drives the portfolio builder? Many emerging leaders are drawn to investing because they are fascinated by new industries, especially disruptive technology. If they can't involve themselves in tech directly through the existing family enterprise, investing is the easiest way for them to participate. Among Chinese business families in particular, rising generation members are often the ones taking care of investments. This is because they have direct exposure to a global investing environment and a strong network, since they were educated outside China and/or are more in touch with newer industries in China like private equity. Many Chinese emerging leaders take this path because they don't want to operate their family's traditional business, especially if it involves spending much of their time in factories located in unattractive second- or third-tier cities or industrial zones.

Moving capital outside the family's operating business is no longer driven primarily by a desire for capital preservation through diversification, as once was the case. Rising leaders are often interested in growing their capital fast through investments in disruptive technology. Capital allocation outside the core business is intended for high growth.

A good example is Gerald Chan. He is the son of T.H. Chan, founder of the Hang Lung Group, a leading Hong Kong real estate developer. While his brother Ronnie stayed in Hong Kong to run the family's legacy business, Gerald studied Medical Radiological Physics and Radiation Biology at Harvard University. Afterwards, he stayed on in the Greater Boston Area and in 1987 started investing locally in both biotech and real estate. It's a clever way to diversify the family real estate business geographically and also invest in a growth industry that reflects his own interests.[14] Chan is a prime example of a family leader using his skills as a portfolio builder.

How to Incubate Your Rising Leaders

Consider that your emerging wealth creators have limited time to ramp up their experience before being given senior level responsibilities. Because their ramp-up time is shorter than their peers who aren't part of business families, they need to use their time effectively. There are many challenges your rising leaders may face in an accelerated ramp-up. Seasoned leaders often ask me how to design a training program to ensure that rising intrapreneurs gain business experience quickly. Working outside of the family business, it takes a few years to learn the necessary business skills, depending on project opportunities that arise. Acquiring these basic skills within the family business is also not always easy, either. Their supervising manager might not give a successor the most challenging work, or may not give honest feedback, fearing that they offend either the current leadership or the successor (or both!). Therefore, supervising managers need to be carefully selected and trained before they can succeed at training the rising family business leaders.

For each kind of wealth creator in your rising generation, there are clear and specific strategies you can apply to accelerate their path and increase their chances of success.

Your twenty-somethings in wealth creation need to practice approaching problems on a macro level. All rising family business leaders need to understand that if they are front-runners, either in an existing industry or in an emerging industry, they are competing against themselves. When you are a front-runner it can be hard to set goals, and it's easy to be blindsided by a competitor who comes out of left field. That means you must out-innovate the rest. To do this, emerging leaders must have a solid True North, strong self-reflection skills, and the capacity to see matters from a higher perspective. (This skill set will prove the most challenging to build for entrepreneurs.) This is where elders and external mentors or coaches can add a huge amount of value to the rising generation.

Intrapreneurs need coaching to help them understand what they are supposed to get out of their jobs (either within or outside the family business). Fundamentally, they need to figure out how any company makes money; what are the key components to make that happen; what are the threats to this money-making mechanism; and what are the opportunities to either improve or completely change their money-making paradigm.

For intrapreneurs working within the family business, it's wise to have an innovation project clearly scoped out. Make it somewhat independent of the regular operations of the family company. This sets your intrapreneur up to build a new bridge from the outside, bringing in new blood for renewal, and helps them to create their own track record much faster. One family I work with are leaders in the food business, making traditional noodles through their mid-tier brand. Their rising twenty-something leader wanted to take the company's products into higher-end brand positioning that appeals to millennials. His goal is to develop products that are more aligned with the health concerns and tastes of younger consumers. The young man and his father, the founder, came up with a solution. The rising leader created a new joint venture between the legacy business and a food branding company so they could jointly create a new brand and product. The legacy company owns the majority; plus, the rising intrapreneur and the outside company both have equity in the new brand. This is the perfect solution, giving the intrapreneur clear recognition and reward for his achievements and helping him learn how to work with the core family company, while benefiting the legacy business in bringing it new growth opportunities.[15]

Given the high failure rate of start-ups, your emerging entrepreneurs will need mentors to advise them on ways to design business models, scale up, build a brand, and promote effectively. Their secret weapon can be the family's network and resources. The family enterprise can offer resources that accelerate and increase their chance of success. This is where centerprising can really help—by using the family enterprise to help the rising entrepreneur create their own gear and link its success to the core. Consider building a talent incubator gear in your Quantum Machine so you can curate these resources for the rising entrepreneur.

Your rising portfolio builders need a crash course in selecting the right areas to invest in. Ben Goldsmith, like many successful British financiers, never even went to university. He jumped right into investing after Eton College. Expert mentors can help your own rising leaders become savvy at selecting the right industries of focus and how to judge probability of successful investment, including quality of team, areas of focus for due diligence, investment terms negotiations, finalizing investment transactions, and supporting portfolio companies after the deal is done. VC, private equity, and other investing jobs are hard to come by, and your rising portfolio builder might not be able to land one. Often, these lessons need to be taught through experience as they go through the process. Some family enterprises create customized programs, structured as internships, to support these activities. The upside for the family enterprise is that it will gain experience in other industries outside of their core businesses and spot opportunities to create new wealth engines. The downside is, they may be isolating for the rising leader. Consider basing a customized program in a global financial center, or at least one germane to their area of special interest, and encourage the portfolio builder to nurture relationships and grow social capital. Warren Buffet reports that he spends 80% of his day reading.[16] In the early days of his career, according to biographer Charles Morris, Buffett relied on the social network he built in business school—which today's portfolio builder is more likely to forego.[17] Young portfolio builders will need your help to strike the balance they need to create effective gears in the family ecosphere.

Harness Their Passion

It truly doesn't matter what type of wealth creator your next-generation member is—internal motivation and most likely eventual success through persistence can only be sustained by real passion. Let your twenty-something feel free to pursue their passions, and then design engagement or roles within your family enterprise that fit with their interests, activities, and willingness to commit.

Even if a rising leader's passion project doesn't initially seem to lead to wealth creation, the family enterprise can centerprise and guide them by asking important questions such as—what value will be accreted to the family enterprise from this venture? Financial value? IP value? Brand value? Social capital? How long will it take, and how much investment is needed? This can challenge them to design a sustainable model with concrete benefits that would accrete to the family enterprise in such ways that it is compelling for the family to support these innovative ventures.

Passion was certainly the driving force behind brothers Stan and FK Day when they established SRAM, a bicycle component manufacturer. The Day brothers (from the Weyerhaeuser timber family) were both keen cyclists who saw a need for a better design for bicycle gears. They started in 1987 with a single product, and eventually grew the SRAM company to become the leading manufacturer of high-end bicycle components in the U.S. Passion stepped in again in 2005 in the wake of the Indian Ocean tsunami. FK Day conceived of a bicycle program that would give people access to education, health care, and economic opportunity. So, FK Day created World Bicycle Relief,[18] a larger organization that eventually became SRAM's major customer and made a significant contribution to SRAM's financial success. The capital this family put into supporting a social enterprise enhanced the SRAM brand and had a financial payoff.[19]

Conclusion

The three greatest lessons an ambitious twenty-something can learn are these: be curious, experiment often, and fail smartly. This is a cycle, and your job is to lead your twenty-somethings through that entire cycle perhaps a few times to develop "muscle memory" to last them a lifetime.

This phase of their life is all about exploration and experimentation. If there is no failure, did they take enough risks? That question will haunt them—and you—forever. Prevent that sense of regret from being part of your business family's story by mobilizing your financial capital, your social network, and your moral authority to propel your emerging wealth creators in their endeavors.

Want to learn how to get your indecisive ownership group to commit? Wonder how other organizations hug the porcupine—embracing their prickly entrepreneur and dealing with the dissonance? Visit centerprising.org

CHAPTER **8**

Getting to Yes with Thirty-Somethings

Taking up the torch is the riskiest decision you'll ever make. At best, it's a leap of faith.

Make no mistake: the stakes are high for your thirty-somethings. During this period, many if not most family members are starting to settle down. This involves committing to life partners, maybe getting married and having kids, choosing a place to live, and finding the right work environment—one that excites them.

The groundbreaking work of psychologist Erik Erikson is particularly useful in understanding adults in their thirties. Even better, Erikson's insights about this stage of life correlate closely with the findings in the Harvard Grant and Glueck studies.

Best known for coining the phrase "identity crisis," Erikson developed a theory of psychosocial development based on eight distinct stages in life. Each stage has its challenges and opportunities. According to Erikson's model, thirty-somethings are in the "Intimacy versus Isolation" stage. Their challenge is how to form loving, meaningful relationships with others.[1] If you want to cultivate good (better still, great) leaders in their thirties, it's useful to think about their development in holistic terms.

Two distinct phases come with the territory for those on this path between the ages of thirty-one and forty. The nesting phase (symbolized by the honeymoon) is a critical period of calm and intimacy required for people to cement their marital (or non-marital) and household commitments. It generally lasts a few years. During this period, family members of origin (like brothers, sisters, parents, and grandparents) can expect tensions around assimilating their new in-laws. You, along with co-workers or managers, may also have difficulties getting the attention of your thirty-something. When nesting, a naturally extroverted and sociable thirty-something may turn into a homebody for some time.

The young family phase is another critical period, sometimes lasting several years, when thirty-something parents of young children are overwhelmed by responsibility and torn by competing demands on their time and emotional bandwidth. During this period, you may watch helplessly as your thirty-something in the business family grows increasingly stressed and struggles for job satisfaction. You will almost always see a dip in performance or productivity at work, and you may begin to see fractures in some core relationships, like marriage or other family relationships, because of too many equally pressing commitments.

Both of these life stages imperil thirty-somethings. Success leads to strong relationships, while failure can lead to loneliness and isolation.

It is tricky to navigate the career plans of next-generation family members in this context of personal development in their thirties. Now that they may be married with children, they will naturally take more people into consideration when making major decisions. Paradoxically, for every motivated and ambitious next-generation member, the desire to be independent increases throughout this time. They want to be paid their worth on the job. They want to validate their own judgment. They want to build their own wealth. They want more authority to make decisions. The search for meaning generally starts here. Now they aim for meaningful accomplishments, not just success for success' sake. Finally, they need due recognition to give them this sense of achievement and to build their own reputation. Your impatient thirty-something will likely want you to clarify their career path. And they will be equally impatient to make a difference in the world.

The Clash Between Elders and Successors

Meanwhile, the senior leaders may not yet be ready to hand over the reins. Typically in their sixties or seventies when rising leaders start cruising through their thirties, elders know they need to start thinking in earnest about succession. They're experiencing their own internal tensions, caught between ambition to achieve the next big goal in their organization and desire to shed the burden of the business and transition to a more relaxed life. The senior leader may be wondering, "What will I do after I retire from working full time at the family company?" They experienced "empty nest syndrome" at home before, when their children moved away to attend college. They may not want to experience it again in their business life.

This can lead to a crisis for senior leaders. The company may well have been their whole life, the baby they have nurtured from day one. It's never easy to step aside, especially if you have doubts about whether the next generation is capable enough to take over, or if you've ever clashed with them over the right way to address high-level issues such as technology disruptions and industry changes.

Based on John Davis' research on work relationships between father–son pairs in family enterprises, the interaction between thirty-something next generation members and their senior generation members can be stormy indeed.[2] Research data confirms that the senior generation is not in any hurry to step aside, while the rising family leader is very much in a hurry to clarify their career trajectory, scope of responsibilities, decision making authority, expectations for delivering results, and the rewards they can expect for their accomplishments in the family enterprise. The Murdoch family empire is a case in point.

In 2018, eighty-seven-year-old media baron Rupert Murdoch was still a controversial decision maker, set to acquire Sky TV (U.K.) in what Bloomberg calls "the media M&A battle of the decade."[3] As many analysts have pointed out, the biggest stumbling block to the ongoing deal still appears to be the leadership of Murdoch himself, who has presided over ethics scandals that are troubling to British regulators. Murdoch's capable children have been working in the family companies for many years and perhaps a leadership transition should have already taken place.

Following best practices, and confirmed by my advisory work, current family leaders need to develop the vision of the ultimate roles and responsibilities each rising family talent can potentially assume. Will they have a seat at the table influencing strategic business issues; ownership issues; or family issues as they relate to the business, such as family employment policy? This will inform how the rising leader would be prepared to succeed in these roles.

After defining future roles, elders and thirty-somethings must form a collaboration that is strong enough to weather the stormy decade ahead. Specifically, you need to decide two things collectively:

1. What role (or roles) is the rising leader likely to play in your family enterprise, and will it be part-time or full-time?; and

2. Will the rising leader have a seat at the table in one or more of the business, ownership, and family forums?

Making a Successful Entry

Negotiating a successful entry into the family enterprise is more than half the battle in developing effective rising-generation wealth creators in their thirties. With highly motivated and talented individuals, you have only to put in the right structure and give them the space to perform. Then they will naturally commit because of their longevity DNA.

You can build your structure easily with a directed, intentional process. That structure has three primary components:

1. *Flexibility* for rising leaders to move into different roles;

2. *Clarity* on the ultimate position(s) that are available to family talent; and

3. *Well-designed compensation packages* that are presented with full transparency.

Flexible roles for wealth creators

There are certain roles—such as wealth creator roles—where it is always best to have multiple next-generation members engaged, whether as intrapreneur, entrepreneur, or portfolio investor. These wealth creator roles tend to be fluid: family business leaders may start as one type of wealth creator, then later evolve to play other wealth creator roles. To expand on our example above, Rupert Murdoch is an excellent illustration of this. The son of a newspaper owner, he had always expected to play a part in the family business: "I was brought up in a newspaper man's home … I saw that life at close range and, after the age of ten or twelve, never really considered any other."[4] After his father's unexpected death in 1952, Rupert took over the running of News Corp Australia (then known as News Limited), becoming managing director at the age of twenty-two. So, the intrapreneur became a portfolio builder, expanding and diversifying the business interests of the company his father had built. Through a series of strategic acquisitions, over the course of his career Rupert Murdoch grew that small newspaper business into a global media empire.

How high can I reach?

A specific consideration for intrapreneurs is what positions to which they can aspire in the family enterprise or ecosphere. This defines their career potential. Philosophies differ for selecting the

CEO and/or chairman of a family business. As an advisor, I have seen a wide range of philosophies, but it is important to consciously decide which one to pursue. Here are three mutually exclusive guiding principles that I have seen applied effectively in different circumstances:

1. "The CEO/chairman should be a family member if there is one with adequate skills, even if there are more talented non-family executives in the company." This works as long as the family CEO knows how to use and incentivize the best non-family talent.

2. "We will select the most talented candidate, regardless of whether they are family or non-family. However, if there is an equally talented family and non-family candidate, preference would be given to family." This can incentivize both family and non-family managers with the possibility of rising to senior management. But if the family member doesn't make it to the top, handle them with care if they decide to stay in the business, and if they decide to leave, handle their exit with equal care.

3. "We will only consider non-family." That position avoids family conflicts, but might make family members less engaged in wealth creation within the existing businesses over time.

On the family wealth level apart from the operating businesses, you need to create opportunities to engage talented entrepreneurs and portfolio builders. An effective approach is to create a family ecosphere that can link the wealth creation activities of all family members to the family enterprise.

How to get compensation right

When structuring compensation packages for your family wealth creators, strive for high transparency paired with good design. This will minimize conflict. Compensation is tricky, and most family enterprises don't get it right. Here are three problematic practices that I often encounter.

The Equality Fallacy: "All family members working in the family company receive the same compensation, regardless of experience, performance, or seniority of role, because the senior generation believes that is the way to make the next generation feel equally treated." The equality principle that might be natural in family and ownership interactions should not always apply in business. Compensation in business should be determined by experience and performance. The danger of an equal compensation practice is that the job and the compensation become a birthright. If there is also a principle (either spoken or unspoken) that you cannot fire family employees, this sense of entitlement can create complacency, increase family conflict, and perhaps lead to political fiefdoms, where seniority gets disconnected from individual performance.

The Favored Few: "Family members receive generous, above-market annual compensation from the family business, though compensation levels are differentiated by seniority, experience, and sometimes (but rarely) performance." The advantage is that family members feel they are being valued by the family enterprise. But if you set the compensation level so much above market, it may provide adverse incentives, such as attracting non-competitive family members who are primarily motivated by the high compensation.

With the "favored few" compensation philosophy, non-family employees will be acutely aware of the preferential treatment that family employees receive. This accentuates the glass ceiling they face. It is often better for the family business to pay market compensation to family employees, based on profit & loss (P & L). Any above-market compensation should ideally be paid from the ownership circle through a trust, family office, or other paths. Fundamentally, it really is a family ownership matter to give extra financial incentives to the family employees.

The Family Sacrifice: "The senior generation views working for the family enterprise as a responsibility and a required sacrifice that dutiful rising-generation members should willingly take on. For that reason, they pay family members less than their market worth." We have seen how this approach creates resentment.

If leaders have no time or ability to build their own wealth, independent of the family, some might start to wonder why they are working so hard to make money for the group while other family members are enjoying their lives and the fruits of the leader's labor. Over time, many of these family leaders will lose motivation.

That resentment has real financial consequences. Emerging generation members stuck in the "family sacrifice" trap go to work every day unhappy. After working for the family over a long period, it's difficult for them to find opportunities elsewhere. They grow less and less motivated to do well or try hard at work. As a result, family wealth creation slows. Family relationships suffer as well, with rising and unresolved tension.

In my work with family businesses, I often come across thirty-somethings who feel uncomfortable with openly discussing their career path and compensation ideas with their elders (whether they be their own parents or uncles, aunts, or cousins) for fear of jeopardizing family relationships. Rather than face difficult conversations, many would prefer to go and work somewhere outside their family business. This is a lost opportunity to capture precious family talent. Senior leaders should take the initiative in setting up these conversations early on, so that both sides are comfortable in expressing their desires and goals freely.

Wealth Creators and the Equity Upside

Consider the story of an entrepreneurial nineteen-year-old European transformed by his gap year experience in Africa doing humanitarian work. When Danish LifeStraw founder Mikkel Vestergaard came back to the struggling family apparel business, Vestergaard Frandsen, with a groundbreaking invention, he asked his father for equity in the company, where he planned to develop his invention. Founder Torben Vestergaard gave an extraordinary answer. If Mikkel was going to transform the company, Torben reasoned, his son needed to lead it. And to lead it decisively, he needed ownership control. Accordingly, Mikkel took the reins, shutting down apparel operations to focus on the social mission of the enterprise. Today, the Lausanne-based maker of LifeStraw, PermaNet, and ZeroFly is a global leader in public health tools. It has won prestigious awards for innovation. CEO Mikkel Vestergaard has publicly challenged himself to conceive of one new life-saving invention every year.[5]

But Mikkel, the emerging-generation entrepreneur, isn't the only visionary responsible for Lifestraw's growth. Torben, his predecessor, gets credit for being a visionary owner, one who can see the future and is willing to empower the next generation to get there. Torben understood that empowerment means giving both management and ownership control.

"Upside" will be a common ask from all three types of wealth creators. They will want you to compensate them with ownership equity and equity-based performance incentives. Most wealth creators don't want to create wealth only for the family at large. To them, that feels unfair. Their jobs are already quite stressful (if they really are performing well), and they are on the receiving end of a lot of pressure from family owners. When things don't go well, they're the ones who get blamed. So, if they don't get more upside than a regular family owner, few feel compelled to perform. It is up to the senior leaders to figure out a way to reward wealth creators with equity the wealth creator feels incentivized.

As a side note, giving ownership stakes (or other similar arrangements) to rising entrepreneurs who build successful ventures will usually lead to unequal wealth among family members. So, a family culture where status is dependent neither on wealth nor power is essential. Make this a bedrock principle when evolving your family ecosphere. Here's a useful tip. When you elevate status in your family based on how much time (or other measurable resources) somebody contributes to the family or to society at large, you are signaling that wealth creation is only one among several ways of creating value.

An Abundance of Wealth Creators
Ready to Lead at Rothschild

What if you wake up one morning and find that you have more than one high-aptitude wealth creator in your family ready to lead? This happened in the Rothschild family in the 1970s. Two cousins, both working in the London bank, had proved their talent for creating value. Sir Evelyn de Rothschild was an intrapreneur. Jacob, Lord Rothschild, was an entrepreneur.

Each cousin respected the other, but which man should run the fabled partnership, N M Rothschild & Sons? A test of wills between the two men turned into a standoff in the business.

Rothschilds was a partnership of equals. All the owners worked in the firm. There was no senior leader, no ownership council, no family council to resolve the impasse. Jacob eventually left the bank to start his own successful financial services business, deepening a divide that already existed within the Rothschild clan. Evelyn stayed on to run the London bank. In retrospect, both cousins regretted their split.[6]

As a result, each man began to focus on how to bring the family back together again using their own respective wealth strategies.

Evelyn's centered around transforming the underperforming legacy business. The London and Paris family banking businesses had been severed during the Second World War. In 1984, Evelyn saw an opportunity after France nationalized Banque Rothschild, putting Evelyn's young French cousin, David René de Rothschild, out of a job. As David struggled with his cousin Eric to rebuild the bank from scratch under the name Rothschild et Compagnie, Evelyn suggested that they begin to work on joint projects. Soon Evelyn was grooming David as his successor. When he made David a partner in the English bank, Evelyn de Rothschild laid the groundwork for reuniting the two family businesses. "The first important strength of the family is unity," Evelyn told *The New York Times* in 1996. "As you sit here and you talk to me, you are talking to David [in France], and if you talk to David, you are talking to me."[7]

Meanwhile, outside the legacy business, Jacob was executing a broader wealth strategy aimed at bringing all of the far-flung family branches back together through various projects. One of them, Rothschild Investment Trust, went public in 1988 under the name RIT Capital Partners. In 2012, RIT formed a joint venture with Edmond de Rothschild Group, a different family banking business based in Geneva and led by Jacob's cousin Benjamin de Rothschild.[8] That same year Jacob's firm, RIT, took a 37% stake in Rockefeller Financial Services, another family business founded by David Rockefeller. The investment achieved a longtime goal for the Rothschild family bankers—to participate in the American market—that had lain dormant since the 19th century.

Today, the two men who suffered a bitter business "divorce" can proudly claim a single legacy: all Rothschild family owners can now utilize several structures to make investments together.[9]

Having multiple highly talented and highly competitive wealth creators can be a mixed blessing. The upside is that they greatly enhance the family enterprise's wealth creation capability. The downside is that if the relationships among wealth creators or their nuclear families are not handled well, it can lead to tensions in family relationships, increasing conflict, and—at the most extreme level—a rupture within the family. A more distributed system with a strong core and many wealth creation gears attached to it led by different family members might be the answer in many circumstances. The Mulliez Family of France has a variation of this system that you can learn about.

"Only An Owner"

This chapter has focused mainly on rising leaders who will be actively engaged in the family enterprise or ecosphere, either as wealth creators or serving in governance roles. We can safely assume that these rising leaders will someday be influential owners. But we haven't addressed capable owners who have active lives and careers outside the system. So let's say a few words about them.

These family members are shareholders or beneficiaries with professional lives. Their interests, activities and expertise place them far outside your boundaries. Or maybe they once had a career in the family enteprise, but now they've moved on. Maiden aunts, bachelor uncles, ADD types and ne'er-do-wells have also fallen into this category for centuries. And they often wield huge power and influence, measured in wealth or shareholding or both. But we tend to discount them.

These capable owners are important because they still bring talent and capital that can be captured. There's nothing worse than demeaning these people as "only an owner." It's important to engage them, because they can make great contributions. Among those contributions may be giving rise to future Phoenixes.

Take the example of Alfred Charles de Rothschild (1842-1918). Science was his passion, and sociability was an enduring trait for this eccentric, cultured Englishman known as London's most popular host.[10] He was never inspired by the banking business, and his business partnership at N M Rothschild & Sons was not a quantum success. Alfred did, however, end up making a major contribution to the family legacy—and the world.

Alfred inherited significant wealth in 1879 on the death of his father. This allowed him to indulge his dual passions for West End theater and zoology. But Alfred had a Future-Forward mindset. He bequeathed all his wealth to his talented daughter Almina Herbert, Countess Carnarvon, a glamorous adventurer married to an Egyptologist. Almina was as bold as her father and used her wealth in 1907 to fund the world's most ambitious archaeological excavation in search of the tomb of the ancient Egyptian boy-king, Tutankhamun.

Alfred didn't live to see Almina's success. The Pharoah's tomb was finally opened in 1923, a sensational discovery "exposing artifacts unsurpassed in the history of archaeology."[11] The enduring power of "King Tut" was so strong that, decades later in 1972, the temporary exhibition of these artifacts and mummies became the most successful in British history. The Rothschild family tradition of science and medical research now added archaeology to the knowledge and information gears that comprised their family ecosphere.

Passion for exploration and natural sciences, sparked by Alfred and Almina, persists in the English branch of the Rothschild family today. In 1993, Jacob Rothschild co-founded the Butrint Foundation to undertake a series of high-profile archaeological excavations and surveys, aiming to preserve the ancient Albanian site chronicled by Virgil.[12] The Foundation made grants for environmental and conservation projects through 2016.[13] In July 2010, to raise awareness of ocean pollution, polar explorer, ecologist, and social entrepreneur David Mayer de Rothschild completed the first Pacific crossing of a vessel he designed, built from reclaimed plastic bottles. Rothschild had invented the fully recyclable material, Seretex, himself.[14]

One issue I want to address about ownership is the concern that most families have about creating a sense of entitlement. They worry about weakening their talent pool when they reward passive owners. This attitude is usually unhelpful.

Ownership should ideally come with benefits. There are some who disagree. They say, if you inherited your ownership, you didn't work for it, and so you don't deserve to benefit. Same goes for other passive owners, in their view. This view assumes that work—contributing your human capital—is the only acceptable justification for financial reward.

But this ignores the contributions of social and intellectual capital, not to mention the financial capital that passive investors often contribute. Passive owners in family companies generally cannot sell their shares, except in internal markets. For this reason, they deserve your respect. They should benefit from their ownersip.

Money, in the form of shareholder returns or distributions, is only one way to benefit your owners usefully. Many families provide benefit packages that include financial support for education, cultural projects, social enterprise, and/or "rainy day" funds set aside to compensate for health crises or unemployment. Whatever the benefit package you offer your owner, it should be meaningful.

But benefits should come with clear reponsibilities. As John Davis likes to say, ownership is a job. Capable owners should attain skill levels that are appropriate to their roles. Reliability is important. Owners should attend all meetings and deliver their work consistently. They should communicate willingly and clearly as needed with other owners. They should learn to explain ownership issues patiently to the rising generation. This is all part of their role as family ambassador.

Owners often need formal training. There are executive education programs that address these issues. You can also develop a custom-designed progam with a trusted advisor. Remember that the highest value of any ownership group in the multigenerational enterprise is its capacity to keep enlarging the pool of talent.

Conclusion

Backing the endeavors of your wealth creators in their thirties is well worth the effort and the risk. All leaders in your family enterprise still have a long runway ahead of them, elders and the rising generation alike. Successful transitions to leadership by thirty-somethings can launch more than lifelong careers. It can launch a decade (or more) of flourishing family unity that results from two generations working effectively alongside one another to grow value for the mothership. It can also benefit the wider circle of employees, clients, vendors, and the wider community that look to them for leadership.

How do Phoenixes make the decision to take the helm?
Read about it at centerprising.org

CHAPTER 9

Frictionless Gearing for Quantum Impact

Clawing your way into the future toughens up your survival DNA.

How to Stay Aligned and Future-Focused

How did people get news they could trust in ancient Greece? When Athenian warriors pushed back the Persian invaders at Marathon in 490 B.C., the victory left Athens vulnerable to a sea attack. From the battlefield, they chose their best runner to report the news and warn the city. He covered twenty-four miles in two hours to file his story, then dropped dead of exhaustion. Eyewitness reporting. Timely delivery. Trusted, actionable information. The first marathon was literally front-page news.

If ever there was an industry custom-built for family ownership, it was the newspaper business. People have always needed independent, unbiased news reporting of high integrity. That requirement has consistently been met by family owners who invested in the print journalism business for the long term. Here's what they invested besides money: pride in ownership, sense of shared values, and capacity to balance profits with a social mandate. This has been true around the world and through the centuries. But will it be true in the future?

Family ownership of newspapers prevailed through the late 20th century, and many of the U.S. companies were family owned. Starting in the mid-2000s, the industry started taking heavy losses. Advertising had always been the industry's mainstay. Dot-coms like Craigslist, luring readers with free classified ads, came on the scene around 2000. By the end of the decade, newspaper industry ad revenue was down by three-quarters.[1] It never recovered. Within the span of just a few years, traditional media companies suffered dramatic reductions in their equity values. Several went out of business altogether, vanquished by the disruption of digital media.

Three well-known, national newspaper companies demonstrate three very different outcomes of this technology disruption.

A Tale of Three Newspapers

The Wall Street Journal gathered news from around the world and printed broadsheets across the country. It published international editions and added a weekend edition to attract advertisers. But in 2005 its readership was still largely limited to business leaders over age fifty-five.[2] The steady decline in value had shrunk the wealth of the Bancroft family owners. In 2007 the Bancrofts united around the difficult decision to sell Dow Jones, the publisher of *The Wall Street Journal*, to another family company, Rupert Murdoch's News Corporation, for $60 a share[3] (67% above Dow Jones's share price when it became public in 1963).[4] Crawford Hill, a member of the Bancroft family, wrote a long and detailed letter at the time of the sale: "We are paying the price of our passivity over the past twenty-five years."[5] (That letter is well worth reading in full for its frank portrayal of a family that failed to engage its rising generation. Nevertheless, they sold at the right time. The industry continued to deteriorate.)

The Washington Post was a local newspaper with a national reach, thanks to its location in the U.S. Capitol and expertise in political reporting. It won acclaim for being first to break the news about the Pentagon Papers and Watergate during the Nixon era. But the company never expanded production nationwide, like its competitors. This made it expensive to deliver broadsheets to subscribers outside the Metro D.C. area. It also meant that *The Washington Post* had limited sources of ad revenue, even for the digital edition. After many years of financial pressure, in 2013 the paper's longtime owners, the Graham family, sold it to Jeff Bezos (founder of Amazon) for $250 million. The sale came in the wake of the family questioning whether their small public company was still the best home for the *Post*. Family business leader Don Graham explained, "Our aim was to see if there was a buyer who could give shareholders a fair deal and make the *Post* newspaper stronger in some way." After looking at various offers, the family chose to sell to Bezos, believing he wanted to buy the newspaper for "the right reasons." Bezos had respect for the newspaper and strong ideas about how to fix the flaws, and the technological capacity to do what was needed to boost the *Post* to greatness again.[6]

The New York Times had long been considered the newspaper of record in the U.S. It supported a legendary international news gathering operation that appealed to well-educated subscribers and printed papers nationwide. In 2009, struggling under $1.4 billion in debt, the company secured a $250 million loan from a minority shareholder, Mexican billionaire Carlos Slim, while "clawing its way into the future" of the digital age. The debt converted to publicly-traded, Class A shares. By 2016, Slim's stake was almost equal to that of the Ochs-Sulzberger family owners who controlled The New York Times through its Class B shares.[7] Against the expectations of analysts, the media company survived and is starting to thrive again. Paid subscriptions doubled in 24 months from 2015 to 2017.[8] The rising leadership team of millennial cousins is headed by thirty-eight-year-old A.G. Sulzberger, named publisher in January 2018. By August, the digital division reported 20% growth over the same period in 2017, a healthy pace. Because of that growth, and in spite of continued pressure from declining ad revenues, the company posted second quarter 2018 profits of $24 million on $415 million in revenue.[9]

How can the stories of these three major newspaper operations lead to three such different outcomes? The key differential variable is whether or not the family owners have built an innovation culture that pervades the whole family enterprise.

Over decades, the family owners of *The Wall Street Journal* had accumulated a fleet of trusts as their ownership vehicles. The family stepped back from formal governance and became reliant on non-family trustees to represent them on the company board. The non-family trustees (mostly lawyers) followed the family's core value of high quality journalism. But the Bancrofts themselves were no longer actively stewarding the family enterprise. When rising leaders began to question the company strategy and sought a more active role in governance, they met stiff resistance. The "top down," passive, "old media" culture had already been set in stone. The Bancrofts never got their chance at centerprising.

Under the Graham family owners after the death of legendary publisher-matriarch Katharine Graham, *The Washington Post* was too slow to digitize and tried to weather the storm by relying on profits from its Kaplan education business. It also published the flailing magazine *Newsweek*, but only one next generation member was involved in the business: Katharine Weymouth, trained as a lawyer. In 2008 she became the fifth member of her family to serve as publisher, just as the global financial crisis was getting under-way. That was bad luck. Changes she introduced brought cost savings to the newsroom. They weren't enough to offset the losses in ad revenue. Katharine's team failed to fundamentally change the business model to keep up with the New Digital Age.

Events at the *New York Times* unfolded differently. Two cousins, Sam Dolnick in digital initiatives and A.G. Sulzberger on the news content side, took leadership roles in a digital revolution—supported by all family owners, the board and the executive team—that would either make or break the heavily indebted company. A third cousin, David Perpich, also played a key part in the push into digital subscriptions.[10] Sulzberger in 2014 headed up an internal assessment of the paper's digital efforts so far. "You couldn't read that report and think that the status quo was an option. ... It's not should we change, it's how do we change."[11]

These days the digital division of the Times looks more like a tech company than a newspaper office, with an open plan design and conference rooms where teams camp out for extended periods to get to solutions. The digital subscription rate is high and growing fast. After floundering in execution of their digital strategy for a decade, *The Times* has figured it out. They're now meeting the needs of all different types of educated readers, from the Silent Generation to post-millennials, delivering international content in many forms (text, photographic, video, podcasts, and AR/VR) and on multiple platforms (print, online, apps for smartphones and tablets, and podcast), covering politics, business, sports, advice on smarter living, media and product reviews, food and travel, fashion and tech. Interactivity is up, with quizzes that deliver feedback and online forums that engage subscribers.

At The New York Times Company, the rising family leaders, along with all members of their generation (even those not working in the business) have built an innovation culture with the right combination of four attributes:

1. *Deeply ingrained family values and shared mission over six generations*, related to their work as an enterprise, believing that journalism is a social institution worth defending, even at great expense to the owners. They are committed to upholding a high standard of journalistic practice "without fear or favor." The family believes that it is their mission as a family to provide this to the nation;

2. *A Future-Forward mindset* in search of a new way to engage new generations while traditional print newspapers are dying all around them;

3. *A commitment to search for a new business model that is financially viable*, while continuing to invest in the integrity of their reporting; and

4. *De-emphasis of personal wealth or status* in living a fulfilled life.

These four attributes align the generations. They also arm the Sulzbergers with what it takes to survive in an industry that's in crisis all around them. Their company may be fighting for survival, but the family is firm in its vocation. Only a few years ago, they almost went up in flames. We're watching their Phoenix rising, before our eyes.

Developing these same four attributes in your own rising leaders means not only creating an innovation culture, but evolving it so that your enterprise will endure for generations.

The shelves are stacked with books about how to innovate a product or a service to disrupt an industry. Or how to transform the organization and culture of an entire company. Far less has been written about the best way to transform the culture of social groups like families and their organizations that are built to last over generations, like a family enterprise. They are committed to surviving shocks in their industries over decades and outlasting the competition.

The same organizations that we praise for their enduring stability are the ones that are slow or even reluctant to adapt. But economic forces around the world make it an imperative for enterprising families to adapt faster than ever before. To survive, you will need to learn from the institutions the tech titans have built. That means experiment more and make quicker keep/kill decisions. There's no time to waste.

Why Slow to Adapt?

Once you accept the need to constantly be open to change, which is the most valuable attribute of an innovation culture, adaptation can seem overwhelming. First of all, there are three main kinds of adaptations you'll need to make at any given time.

Maybe your industry is already being disrupted (and your existence is being threatened) by technology you don't understand, and you can see the need to respond with fresh product or service offerings. Or maybe you need to re-envision how you get things done, say in your corporate work environment or your processes. Or what about the need to create trusted relationships with new customers or new stakeholders? The way you do that needs to be authentic, and the story you tell needs to come across as your unique brand culture. You can see all that. But which one comes first?

There are also three levels of innovation. There are small tweaks you can make in the current product or work processes. You can introduce new or improved products that replace existing products, whether founded on the existing product platforms or grown out of an improved biz model that replaces the current ones. Or you can pivot and head in an entirely new direction.

For example, compare Thomas Watson Jr. of IBM with Cristina Stenbeck of Kinnevik, two very different kinds of innovators. Watson, the pioneering inventor, adapted slowly, unthreatened by extinction and open to possibilities, allowing for a natural evolution of his own talents and ideas. He spearheaded the electronic computing technology that replaced punch cards. That was innovation by developing products based on an entirely new technology.

Cristina Stenbeck, a third-generation Swedish family business leader who was only twenty-four when she was named Chairman of the family business, had watched her father do just that by disrupting the British telecom industry. Jan Stenbeck had never been very interested in his father's "old industry" timber and steel conglomerate, A.B. Kinnevik. He was fascinated by new technology.

In 1982 Jan amazed his English business partner when he told him about a new "cellular" technology that could beam a short-wave signal automatically from "cell to cell." The pair pioneered the consumer cell phone in 1982 when Stenbeck bought the U.K.'s second cellular license, founded Vodaphone, and sprinted past the competition before exiting. He then became the first to use satellite technology for TV broadcasting. (Rupert Murdoch's Sky TV battle dates from that first Stenbeck satellite lease.)[12]

Jan's sudden death put Cristina in charge in her mid twenties. Like her father, she was Future-Forward and wanted to stay ahead of the curve in technology. But Christina was not herself a serial pioneer. So, she decided to use financial resources "trapped" in the flagship business (forestry and steel manufacture) to invest in pioneering innovations. Cristina made the decision to sell off all remaining "old industry" assets from Kinnevik's founding days to make investments solely in online ventures. Her way of innovating was to transform the focus of her family enterprise. In 2017, frustrated with "administration" and governance, she stepped down as Chairman of Kinnevik to focus on developing entrepreneurs, naming a non-family manager as her replacement.[13] Wealth creation is not role dependent. Remember, you can get results working in an ownership role, too.

Cristina Stenbeck is an outlier. Family ownership groups are often slow to adapt, even given any or all of these opportunities. Why? There are many good reasons. The long tenure of the family CEO or chairman creates a tendency to hold on to legacy operations and stratagems. Expectations of stable dividends can make family owners so risk averse that they come to see change as a threat, not a reality. As a result, families can be slow to adapt. Status is important in every family, so reserving high status for the business leaders, and nobody else, can lead to major problems—notably, a lack of fresh ideas and new perspectives. Families can also develop an unwillingness to rock the boat with new behavior that might bring family disharmony.

Share the Vision or Lose It

Don't try building an innovation culture without first making sure that the owners share a common or collective vision of the future. That is the first job for any singular leader. Centerprising requires all family members to be both leaders and followers of your vision. Because in any given project, initiative or organization, some leaders are bound to move faster or slower than others. A shared vision means that you'll always be able to coordinate your efforts (while your family members create new gears supported by the family enterprise). And stakeholders won't be confused by mixed messages from different family owners or the family senior management. This is what I call *frictionless gearing*.

A shared vision will help you develop an inspiring, authentic family identity. This will keep you motivated. It will help craft your brand stories, and through those stories you'll create a brand culture that key stakeholders—clients, employees, investors, external partners—can grasp. Consider the iconic origin story of

California blue jeans, patented in 1873 by Levi Strauss, and the brand culture around Levis denim jeans, made by the Haas family owners ever since. The Levis brand is practically synonymous with ideas like "pioneering spirit" and "the American dream." A Levis customer is practically synonymous with "the working man." The Levi Strauss family enterprise thrives in good times and bad for the apparel industry. It is strong enough to weather rough storms in large part because of an authentic identity that little can destroy. If your shared vision isn't compelling enough to inspire everyone in the family, it's probably not relatable for your stakeholders.

In my work with family enterprises, I often see that family members don't spend enough time resolving their differences. So, arriving at a shared vision becomes a challenge. This may be because family members avoid these discussions, fearing that they may lead to conflict. It may also be that everyone is busy with everyday operational tasks. More family owners and senior managers need to carve out time to learn about the latest trends in their own plus adjacent industries. They need time and space to think outside the box and imagine new directions. They need to reflect on the impact of technological disruption to their industries—and to other completely unrelated industries. They need to consider whether it's time to bet new wealth creation on innovations in another totally unrelated industry that just might, under closer examination, compliment or parallel their own. Future-Forward thinking is hard work. And it takes time.

You Can Ride the Waves of Disruption

Around the time of generational transitions, it is critical to do the work of aligning visions between current and rising generation family leaders. Otherwise, current stewards may not feel confident in entrusting their successors with steering the business and the family wealth, and the rising generation may not feel motivated to take over a family enterprise where the vision isn't their own.

Rising generation members often have fresh ideas about how the family enterprise can keep up with technology disruptions and emerging market trends, and how it can take on a more innovation driven and entrepreneurial mindset. Current stewards have valuable insights on running an existing business organization, negotiating, working with government or regulatory agencies, and leveraging their network and resources. Working together, they are a powerful team.

When your industry is going through drastic, speedy, and disruptive changes, alignment comes to the fore. In an industry where players might win or lose fast and in dramatic fashion, the family business needs to mirror the behavior of the start-ups that are emerging to compete with them by being nimble in experimenting with new technology, new processes, and new thinking. Many experiments will lead to failure, but the few that succeed will make you leaders in your industry. Set expectations around failure accordingly. Without genuine buy-in, accusations might start flying about misjudgments, incompetence, wasting money, and more. It could tear the family apart.

When his father passed away in 1998, Ernesto Bertarelli took over ownership of Serono, the family pharmaceutical company. With his sister Dona, Ernesto pivoted the company's focus from pharmaceuticals to biotechnology and diversified their activities into other wealth management. The results were more than pleasing: they expanded revenue to $2.4 billion before selling it to Merck in 2007 for over $13 billion.[14]

There is a perfect storm in many family enterprises as new technology (AI, big data, robotics, genetic engineering, and more) is upending traditional industries, just as we are in the midst of the biggest generational wealth transfer of recent times with baby boomers retiring en masse. The good news is that this "perfect storm" can generate the kind of energy that propels a family enterprise to dominance in its sector. We see this at The *New York Times*, where the family-led leadership team is investing heavily in a core offering (journalism, in this case) while adding steadily to their array of digital services and features, such as a personalized news reader. Their goal is no longer to maximize revenue from advertising: it's to make subscriptions the wealth engine of a billion-dollar business.

Building Your Authentic Brand Culture

As you work on defining and clearly articulating the core values for your family enterprise, think of them as being the tributaries that feed into a single mighty river. That river then irrigates the land all around it, yielding consistent harvests year after year. That land-scape thus created is your authentic brand culture, the way your values are made tangible for your consumers, your employees, and all of your other key stakeholders.

Both brand and innovation cultures are key to success in today's industries, where technological disruption abounds and millenni-als dominate the consumer and work cultures. Your authentic brand culture enables the public to have a deep, intimate emotional rela-tionship with your organization, and as a result they will become customers who are devoted to your products or services. The stron-ger a brand's perceived authenticity, the more likely people are to become advocates for it.[15]

We see that family enterprises with the greatest success in trans-forming themselves, and thus building an authentic brand culture, are the ones where the next-generation leaders have spearheaded the effort to define what the family stands for. These next-genera-tion members are passionate and able to garner the support of other family members to adopt a specific brand culture that authentically represents the family enterprise's core values. The key word here is "authentic": in order to represent well, family members need to talk the talk and walk the walk, never viewing it as a cynical exercise in grabbing market share.

The grandfather of all-American brands is Levi Strauss, endur-ing since 1853 and making Coca-Cola and Ford (founded in 1892 and 1903 respectively) seem like relative newcomers. Today, such is the width and depth of its authenticity that Levi Strauss is described as a "brand titan," appealing to men and women, young and old, rich and poor, conservative and counter-cultural alike.[16] More than the denim itself, the company is known for tak-ing a stand on social responsibility issues. Back in the 1890s, Levi Strauss established scholarships for students at the University of California, Berkeley. Ever since then, the company has pursued a mission that its leadership group calls "profits through principles." Through its innovative Water-Less™ finishing techniques, devel-oped in 2011, the company has saved more than a billion liters of water, sharing its methods to encourage water conservation across the apparel industry.

More than any other type of business, family enterprises have unique opportunities to create this authentic brand culture. The family owners are naturally seen by outsiders to embody the family enterprise brand image. Rising generation members in particular have opportunities to blend strong family values with entrepreneurial values, together with prevailing values of the current times. The result is a renewed and renewable family brand that carries the family's longstanding DNA, just expressed a little differently in every generation. Only the rising generation is able to do that. This is the most compelling reason of all why the senior generation should consider empowering their Phoenixes as a strategy to grow and profit from new industry trends.

Adaptation for Wealth Creators of All Kinds

Your innovation culture is equally relevant to all of the wealth creators in your family enterprise, even though it will be demonstrated in different ways.

The entrepreneurs in your family, who are being supported at the edge until their ventures take off with a viable business model, will often be at the forefront of change and shifting stakeholder demands. Listen to them carefully and maybe even start the process of assimilating their brand culture, if it links in with the family enterprise's mission.

The portfolio builders in your family scan their horizons and see a lot of investment flow. Driving that are a multitude of different persepctives about disruptive change and opportunity. Your star capital allocators may not be committed to one brand culture or any single emerging business model, but they are a great source of information. Turn to them, engage them, as catalysts for new thinking.

Your entrepreneurially-minded intrapreneurs almost always deserve special care. Seniors, don't assume that they aren't paying attention or that they're not learning. You could easily end up like Samuel du Pont, who pushed his son away. Samuel never got to work alongside Pierre, who had quietly become a master craftsman during his teenage period of experimentation. Samuel never appreciated his son's talent until the day Pierre handed him a priceless watch and walked away forever. Your intrapreneurs may spearhead the transformation of the legacy business. They may achieve it by developing new products or services; introducing a new business model for existing products or services; or entering into an entirely new industry.

Conclusion

It will take a great deal of wisdom from the senior generation in your business family to understand how to work with all the rising leaders in the emerging generation and stoke their individual passions. Once that evolved DNA takes hold, it will pay back generously over the generations to come.

CHAPTER **10**

Spotting the Stars

Success is not final, failure is not fatal: it is the courage to continue that counts.

Winston Churchill

This book has been about enterprising families—the way their enterprises have evolved, are evolving today and can evolve better in the future—for their own benefit and the benefit of all communities they touch.

If you're the seasoned leader of a non-family organization and you've read this far, looking for insights on how to spot and develop Phoenixes who will transform your own organization or institution, I congratulate you on your persistence. Like your counterparts in family business, you've chosen to work with a team of people and stakeholders whom you care deeply about. They're your family. When you draw your last breath as a leader, they're the ones you want beside you, holding your hand. They're the ones who matter to you.

But is the converse true? Do you matter to them?

Through my family business advisory work with business families where I often hold one-on-one discussions with all family members young and old, I can assure you that you do matter to them. You matter because you're the protector of critical shared resources. You've been replenishing those resources for your entire career, as reliably as any leader who opens the water gates to replenish the mill pond in their ecosphere. You matter because of your dedication to the shared vision, values, and mission. You matter because of your deep respect for team members as human beings with individual identities. That is what drove your daily efforts over decades. You have shown the world how stable and strong the collective resources are.

For all these reasons and more, you do matter to the rising generation ... more than you know. They need a strong connection with you. They need your validation. They need your sponsorship.

Without it, the starting forces that you can help to multiply will be greatly diminished. And sometimes this will be fatal for them.

Think about two Phoenixes profiled in this book, Alexandre Birman and Irénée du Pont. Both innovators had to succeed according to their own plan. For Birman and du Pont, the difference in preparation was in the unforced errors by the senior leader. When Alexandre went to his father for a loan, his father wrote him a cheque. Irénée needed to find a non-family sponsor and even an adversarial partner for his business plan because his father never really believed in him. Which senior leader, which parent, do you want to be?

In the end, Pierre du Pont died helping his son put out a fire in the Eleutherian Mills. They never had the best relationship. As hard as seasoned leaders might resist the notion, the Longevity DNA that forged you into the leader you are today is something that most human beings with horizons like yours will choose, in the end, to replenish and instill in others. Even with their last breaths.

If not … consider your fate—the worst fate of all: losing relevance. This is what Percy Bysshe Shelley describes so well in his poem *Ozymandias*,[1] written when he was only 26, already so aware (like many millennials today) of the fate of history and the ravages of time:

> I met a traveler from an antique land,
> Who said—"Two vast and trunkless legs of stone
> Stand in the desert … Near them, on the sand,
> Half sunk a shattered visage lies, whose frown,
> And wrinkled lip, and sneer of cold command,
> Tell that its sculptor well those passions read
> Which yet survive, stamped on these lifeless things,
> The hand that mocked them, and the heart that fed;
> And on the pedestal, these words appear:
> My name is Ozymandias, King of Kings;
> Look on my Works, ye Mighty, and despair!
> Nothing beside remains. Round the decay
> Of that colossal Wreck, boundless and bare
> The lone and level sands stretch far away.

Percy Bysshe Shelley

For seasoned leaders, it's time for practical matters. If you're leading a non-family organization and you agree that long-term thinking is vital to its survival, you face a decision.

If you're leading a family enterprise and agree that disruption threatens your relevance in the new economy, and maybe even your survival in the next generation, you face a decision.

Organizations are not the source of Longevity DNA. People are. Organizations are not the inspiration for long-term thinking that can shape the governance needed in a distributed economy. People are. Organizations are not the ground zero of creative disruption. People are. Organizations are there to help people thrive. It's innovators in whom we need to make our investments. I hope you will decide to use your own pioneer spirit to help people thrive, first and foremost, above and beyond organizations. To stay relevant, focus on developing your people.

One of my mentors told me when I was in college that it is impossible to go against the tide of history. Your decision is whether to stay relevant by (1) leading transformation of mindsets, (2) developing and engaging all your rising generation members as leaders, plus (3) designing an interdependent ecosphere for your family and building a Quantum Machine.

It's time to pause and consider what to do next. I understand those of you who wonder why you should undertake all these new challenges. Haven't you already proven yourself in building the business, which is why you're now collecting accolades? Those laurels are good for the family, right? So why not enjoy basking in the limelight that is yours by right—and well deserved?

Or maybe you've gained the perspective of a seasoned leader, but you still feel that you haven't accomplished enough. This emotion probably runs deepest for those of you whose forbearers lived long lives and held lifelong leadership tenures. It's even worse when your predecessor was a legend. How do you top that? Have you only recently (or maybe not even yet) received full ownership of the resources you have been stewarding for a long time? For most of your adult lives, you were saddled with "responsibility without authority," like Prince Charles—still a prince, not a king, at age seventy. It's natural to want to put your own stamp on history.

You want your best days to be ahead of you. There's still stuff left to do on your own agenda. Why lose that momentum to turn around and focus attention on the rising generation? Why can't they struggle forward on their own? Why do you have to be the one to lead them through this period of disruption? Finally, the realities of physically getting older mean you move slower in shrinking activity circles. It takes longer to do everything, and daily life generally gets more frustrating. While you're only just learning to be patient with yourself, you're now being asked to learn to be patient with the rambunctious bunch who aim to take your place, make you irrelevant, and who think that everything you do is so yesterday. Why do this to yourself? Why put yourself through it?

When you imagine starting over ... charting new waters with the rising leaders and lending a helping hand to their labors. ... let's face it, you may even fail at this new role. Making mega-million dollar acquisitions? That you can do. Listening to the rising leader make the case of why to upend the current business model? That ... you're not so sure. Is that really something you want to take on, when you can exit the stage with a bang, having fun?

Before writing this book, I spent a lot of time with seasoned leaders in the senior generation. I wanted to understand how they framed the challenges they face, what they worry about, and what they think of rising leaders in the next generation. I haven't stopped listening, and I never plan to stop. So, as I listen to them closely and repeatedly, a few themes emerge:

> *"They have accomplished so much more at their age than we did when we were that age."*

> *"I am in awe of what they can do with technology."*

> *"I wish they would take more risks and think about what the business will become in fifteen to twenty years."*

> *"Why don't they seem very engaged? They come in at ten and leave at six. How can they look after the troops that way?"*

> *"I think they still have a lot to learn, but they don't realize it."*

> *"What if one careless fall proves to be fatal?"*

For rising leaders reading these comments, I hope they resonate. Senior leaders are thinking about you. You're what keeps them up at night. They don't have the heart to ask you what they really want to know. Like: are you just trying your luck, or do you bring mastery to your new ventures? They search for the words to tell you what Alex Honnold, at age thirty-three the only person in the world to have free soloed El Capitan, expresses so well: "I didn't want to be a lucky climber. I want to be a great climber."[2] Luck can run out. And that is when fatal accidents happen.

Mastery does not have to stifle creativity. Part of creative mastery is being very, very prepared in whatever you do. If you take anything away from this book, rising leaders, I'd like you to come to seniors for resources on your new projects confident in how prepared you are—ready to report how you listened to different perspectives and considered the risks. "Be prepared" isn't just a Boy Scout motto. It's how you should approach every innovation because luck will happen. Whether it's good luck or bad luck, the unforeseen will happen to you in business and in life. Being prepared, like Alex Honnold, is making a commitment to eliminate every possible unforced error.

For seasoned leaders, it's time to double down on that commitment. You need to eliminate unforced errors, too. Change is inevitable, but transformation must be intentional. Innovating on the fringe to replenish the core is a good strategy for the future in a distributed world economy.

It's worth taking inspiration from the royal house of Windsor with a legendary global leader Queen Elizabeth II at the helm of a family ecosphere, operating an international governance organization that has impacted British subjects for a thousand years. Disruption could have global consequences by breaking up the "family firm," known as the Commonwealth Nations. On May 19, 2018, the Windsor family and several rising leaders, including Prince Charles, held a high-visibility event to signal replenishing of the family mill pond—which also signaled the stability and strength of its resources. The wedding of Meghan Markle and Prince Harry was a quantum event with global impact, sending messages about the transformation of the brand through a new ethos that has been adopted as cutting-edge by youthful audiences around the world. Already there's evidence that this innovative approach to cultural change is warmly received by citizens of the Commonwealth Nations. "Suddenly," wrote a journalist about the Sussexes' Australian tour to promote the Invictus Games, "the house of Windsor has become incredibly relevant."[3]

Remember: You matter to them, more than you know.

And also keep in mind: you can't tell, in advance, which rising leaders will turn into Phoenixes.

So, you've got to develop as many as you can and keep an open mind.

Because even on the darkest night, you can't always see the stars.

Notes

Preface

1. Lee, B. 2002. *Striking Thoughts: Bruce Lee's Wisdom for Daily Living.* New York: Tuttle Publishing.

2. Hoffman, R. *How to build your company to last: John Elkann, Chair of Fiat Chrysler Automobiles.* Masters of Scale Episode 18 (podcast). Transcript at https://mastersofscale.com (accessed October 31, 2018).

3. "Dynasty" calls. *The Economist.* May 8, 2008.

4. Orange, M. 2012. *Rothschild: Une banque au pouvoir.* Paris: Albin Michel, p. 12.

5. Runciman, D. 2018. "China's Challenge to Democracy." *The Wall Street Journal*, February 26, 2018 https://www.wsj.com/articles/chinas-challenge-to-democracy-1524756755 (accessed January 9, 2019).

6. Lardy, N. 2014. *Markets Over Mao: The Rise of Private Business in China.* Washington, D.C.: Peterson Institute for International Economics.

Chapter 1 Part A

1. "Iron Man." Dir. John Favreau. Perf. Robert Downey, Jr, Gwyneth Paltrow, Terrence Howard and Jeff Bridges. 2008. Paramount Pictures and Marvel Enterprises. DVD.

2. Taleb, Nassim Nicholas. 2012. *Antifragile: Things That Gain from Disorder.* New York: Random House. p. 430.

3. Edelman. 2014. "Edelman Trust Barometer Annual Global Study." Report, Edelman.

4. Halbert, M. L. 2016. "How Alexandre Birman plans to take his success worldwide." *Footwear News.* August 8, 2016. https://footwearnews.com/2016/fashion/designers/inside-alexandre-birman-arezzo-and-company-brazilian-footwear-246636/ (accessed November 1, 2018).

5. Snyder, G. 2017. "Keeping up with the Times: The New York Times claws its way into the future." *Wired.* February 12, 2017. https://www.wired.com/2017/02/new-york-times-digital-journalism/.

6. Bersin, J., McDowell, T., and Rahnema, A. 2017. "The organization of the future: Arriving now." 2017 Global Human Capital Trends. *Deloitte Insights.* February 28, 2017.

7. Frazier-Wall, J. 1990. *Alfred I. Du Pont: The Man and His Family.* New York: Oxford University Press, pp. 25–30.

8. Ibid. pp. 11–12.

9. Ibid. p. 15.

10. Ibid. p. 18.

11. Ibid. p. 19.

12. Ibid. p. 32.

13. Ibid. p. 32.

14. Ibid. p. 37.

15. Ibid. p. 38.

16. Ibid. p. 54.

17. Ibid. p. 44.

18. Gurdus, E. 2018. "Dow Du Pont CEP says split will generate nearly 1 billion in research funding." *CNBC.* November 8, 2108. www.cnbc.com/2018/11/08/dowdupont-ceo-on-company-split-nearly-1-billion-in-research-funding.html (accessed February 18, 2019).

Chapter 1 Part B

1. "Back to the Future." Dir. Robert Zemeckis. Perf. Michael J. Fox, Christopher Lloyd, Lea Thompson. 1985. Universal Pictures. DVD.

2. Popular with millennials, the Warner Bros. trilogy credited with reviving the DC Comics superhero franchise consists of: "Batman Begins." Dir. Christopher Nolan. Perf. Christian Bale, Liam Neeson, Cillian Murphy and Katie Holmes. 2005 Warner Bros. DVD; "The Dark Knight." Dir. Christopher Nolan. Perf. Christian Bale, Heath Ledger and Aaron Eckhart. 2008 Warner Bros. DVD; and "The Dark Knight Rises." Dir. Christopher Nolan. Perf. Christian Bale, Tom Hardy, Anne Hathaway and Marion Cotillard. 2012 Warner Bros. DVD.

3. Davis, J. and Tsai, F. "Strategies for growing multi-generational family wealth." Article on Cambridge Family Enterprise Group website. https://cfeg.com/insights_research/strategies-for-growing-multi-generational-family-wealth (accessed November 5, 2018).

4. Davis, J. 2012 *Enduring Advantage: Collected Essay on Family Enterprise.* Cambridge, Massachusetts: Cambridge Family Enterprise Group. 2012, pp. 1–7.

5. Davis, J. "A tribute to Renato Tagiuri." Cambridge Family Enterprise Group website. https://cfeg.com/about/tagiuri-renato (accessed October 31, 2018).

6. Rojc, P. 2017. "So many Pritzkers, so much philanthropy: Meet this top family of givers." *Inside Philanthropy*. August 17, 2017.

7. Cornil, Y., Crawford, R., and Bennedsen, M. 2015. "The Mulliez Family Venture," INSEAD Business School Case.

8. Based on a real business family, but identifying details have been changed to protect the privacy of individuals.

9. Mayer Amschel Rothschild. Profile in *Forbes*. July 21, 2005.

10. Ferguson, N. *The House of Rothschild: Volume 1: Money's Prophets: 1798-1848*. New York: Penguin Random House, 1999, 544 pp; Ferguson, N. *The House of Rothschild: Volume 2: The World's Banker 1849-1999*. New York: Penguin Random House, 2000, 576 pp.

11. Brodie, S. 2007. "Rothschild dynasty unites after 190 years." *The Telegraph*. July 18, 2007. https://www.telegraph.co.uk/finance/markets/2812381/Rothschild-dynasty-unites-after-190-years.html (accessed October 31, 2018).

12. "RIT Capital Partners, chaired by Lord Rothschild, and Rockefeller & Co. announce strategic partnership." Press release on Cision PR Newswire. May 30, 2012.

13. Scott, M. 2012. "Rockefeller and Rothschild dynasties join forces." *New York Times*. May 30, 2012.

14. McGagh, M. 2017. "Rothschild's RIT Capital sells Rockefeller stake." *Investment Trust Insider*. October 10, 2017.

15. Guo, X. L. 2018. "The Tencent Ecosystem: Half of the value depends on its investments." *The Founder*. February 6, 2018 (in Chinese).

Chapter 2

1. Dyer, D. and Gross, D. 2001. *The Generations of Corning: The Life and Times of a Global Corporation*. New York: Oxford University Press.

2. For more on insider and outsider types in family companies, see Davis, J. 2015. "Developing your next CEO for the family business." Article on the Harvard Business School website. November 24, 2015. https://hbswk.hbs.edu/item/managing-the-family-business-developing-your-next-ceo (accessed November 5, 2018).

3. Marsden, S. 2012. "Agatha Christie's The Mousetrap celebrates its 60th anniversary with star-studded show." *The Telegraph*. November 18, 2012.

4. "The 2017 Edinburgh Festival Fringe draws to a close." Press Release, Edinburgh Festival Fringe Society. August 28, 2017. https://www.edfringe.com/learn/news-and-events/2017-fringe-draws-to-a-close (accessed October 31, 2018).

5. Frisby, D. 2018. "The economics of the Edinburgh Fringe." *Chortle*. August 11, 2018. https://www.chortle.co.uk/correspondents/2018/08/11/40806/the_economics_of_the_edinburgh_fringe.

6. BOP Consulting. 2016. "Edinburgh Festivals 2015 impact study." https://www.edinburghfestivalcity.com/assets/000/001/964/Edinburgh_Festivals_-_2015_Impact_Study_Final_Report_original.pdf?1469537463.

7. Gardner, L. 2017. "'We haven't made a profit for five years': Risky business at Edinburgh Fringe." *The Guardian*. July 19, 2017.

8. "STOMP." By Steve McNicholas and Luke Cresswell. Directed and produced by Steve McNicholas and Luke Cresswell. Performance by Luke Cresswell, Theseus Gerard, Fraser Morrison, Carl Smith, Nick Dwyer, David Olrod and Sarah Eddy. Bloomsbury Theatre, London, 1991.

9. Singh, A. 2015. "West End audiences hit record high thanks to Twitter." *The Daily Telegraph*. June 23, 2015.

10. Snow, G. 2018. "West End audiences top 15 million for the first time, SOLT data reveals." *The Stage*. February 27, 2018.

11. Cox, G. 2017. "Fast-rising prices drive Broadway to $1.6 billion year." *Variety*. December 29, 2017.

12. "About SpaceX." Company website. https://www.spacex.com/about (accessed January 3, 2019).

13. Loria, K. 2018. "The scariest parts of the new climate change report: The goals the world set are inadequate, and the track we're on is disastrous." *Business Insider*. October 8, 2018. https://www.businessinsider.com/ipcc-climate-change-report-why-2-degree-warming-is-dangerous-2018-10.

14. Keenan, J., Hill, T., and Gumber, A. 2018. "Climate gentrification: From theory to empiricism in Miami-Dade County, Florida." *Environmental Research Letters* 13(5). http://iopscience.iop.org/article/10.1088/1748-9326/aabb32/meta (accessed November 6, 2018).

15. Dyer, D. and Gross, D. ibid.

16. Cerami, C. A. 2004. *Jefferson's Great Gamble*. Naperville: Sourcebooks.

17. Krinsky, C. H. 1978. *Rockefeller Center*. New York: Oxford University Press.

Chapter 3

1. Agrawal, A. J. 2016. "Jobs or Gates: Differences in leadership." *Inc.com*. May 5, 2016.

2. "Bill Gates's transactional leadership style." *Daily Mirror*. June 11, 2015.

3. Locker, M. 2017. "Can you guess which tech company has the best corporate culture?" *FastCompany*. November 30, 2017. https://www.fastcompany.com/40502370/can-you-guess-which-tech-company-has-the-best-corporate-culture (accessed January 11, 2019).

4. Forbes Technology Council. 2018. "13 Reasons Google deserves its 'Best Company Culture' award." *Forbes*. February 18, 2018. www.forbes.com/sites/forbestechcouncil/2018/02/08/13-reasons-google-deserves-its-best-company-culture-award/#332ae17e3482 (accessed January 11, 2019).

5. Based on a real case study, but made anonymous to protect the privacy of individuals.

6. Taylor, K. 2017. "40 of the biggest scandals in Uber's history." *Business Insider*. November 24, 2017. www.businessinsider.com/uber-company-scandals-and-controversies-2017-11#february-2017-a-female-engineer-who-used-to-work-at-uber-publishes-a-blog-post-about-sexual-harassment-and-gender-inequality-at-the-company-21 (accessed January 11, 2019).

7. Yurieff, K. 2018. "Uber's HR chief steps down after discrimination probe." *CNN Business*. July 11, 2018. https://money.cnn.com/2018/07/11/technology/uber-hr-head-resigns/index.html (accessed October 31, 2018).

8. Honnold, A. 2018. "How I climbed a 3,000-foot vertical cliff—without ropes." *TED*.

9. Gladwell, M. 2008. "Better to be lucky than good." *TheStreet: Investing Strategies*. November 25, 2008. https://www.youtube.com/watch?v=njdjYI5ciws (accessed February 19, 2019).

10. Gates, Bill. 2010. "A conversation with my father." June 2, 2010. Published May 6, 2011 by FORA TV. www.youtube.com/watch?v=GihiSE6SM (accessed February 19, 2019).

11. Marks, H. 2011. *The Most Important Thing: Uncommon Sense for the Thoughtful Investor*. New York: Columbia University Press, p. 136.

12. Honnold, A. ibid.

13. Gordon, S. and Sanderson, R. 2017. "Agnelli heir makes bet on family fortune." *Financial Times*. April 4, 2017.

14. Sanderson, R. 2011. "Unlikely heir who saved the family jewels." *Financial Times*. March 6, 2011.

15. "Dynasty calls." *The Economist*. May 8, 2008.

Chapter 4

1. Based on a real case study. Names and identifying details have been changed to protect the privacy of individuals.

2. Watson Jr., Thomas and Petre, Peter. *Father, Son & Co.: My Life at IBM and Beyond*. 1990. New York: Bantam Books, page vii.

3. Pink, P. 2009. *Drive: The Surprising Truth of What Motivates Us*. New York: Riverhead Books, 272 pp.

4. Dimock, M. 2018. "Defining Generations: Where Millennials End and post-Millennials Begin." http://www.pewresearch.org/fact-tank/2018/03/01/defining-generations-where-millennials-end-and-post-millennials-begin/ (accessed January 4, 2019).

5. Georgescu, P. 2018. "Just 100 Do Well By Doing Good." https://www.forbes.com/sites/petergeorgescu/2018/01/10/just-100-well-by-doing-good/#680dccda6335 (accessed January 4, 2019)

6. Porter, M. and Kramer, M. 2011. "Creating shared value." *Harvard Business Review* 89(1/2): 62–77, 16 pp.

7. Watson Jr., T. and Petre, P. Ibid., p. ix.

8. Klepper, M. and Gunther, R. *The Wealthy 100: From Benjamin Franklin to Bill Gates—a Ranking of the Richest Americans, Past and Present*. 1996. New York: Citadel Press, 362 pp. A calculation placing him second was made by comparing Vanderbilt's wealth to the gross domestic product. Calculations made in 1998 placed him third: Klepper, M., Gunter, R., Baik, J. Barth, L. and Gibson, C. 1998. "The American Heritage 40; A ranking of the forty wealthiest Americans of all time (Surprise: Only three of them are alive today)." *American Heritage*, Volume 49, Issue 6 Archived December 11, 2007, at the Wayback Machine.

9. Stiles, T.J. *The First Tycoon: The Epic Life of Cornelius Vanderbilt*. 2009. New York: First Vintage Books Edition, p. 121.

10. Ibid., p. 561.

Chapter 5

1. "Citizen Kane." 1941. Dir. Orson Welles. Perf. Orson Welles, Joseph Cotton, Dorothy Comingore. RKO Radio Pictures. DVD.

2. Kilday, G. 2017. San Francisco International Film Festival: William Randolph Hearst III discusses "Citizen Kane." *The Hollywood Reporter*. April 7, 2017. https://www.hollywoodreporter.com/video/william-randolph-hearst-iii-discusses-citizen-kane-992240 (accessed January 5, 2019).

3. Kreamer, A. 2012. "The business case for reading novels." *Harvard Business Review*. January 11, 2012.

4. Vaillant, G. 2012. *Triumphs of Experience: The Men of the Harvard Grant Study*. Cambridge, Mass: The Belknap Press of Harvard University Press, 480 pp.

5. Mineo, L. 2017. "Good genes are nice, but joy is better." *The Harvard Gazette*. April 11, 2017.

6. Bhattacharjee, Y. 2015. "The first year." *National Geographic*. January 2015.

7. Schneidman, L., Gweon, H., Schultz, L. Woodward, A. 2016. "Learning from others and spontaneous exploration: A cross-cultural investigation." *Child Development*, May/June 2016, Vol 87 No. 3 pp. 723-735.

8. Hoffman, K., Cooper, G., and Powell, B. 2017. *Raising a Secure Child*. New York: The Guilford Press.

9. Bergin, C. and Bergin, D. 2009. "Attachment in the classroom." *Educational Psychology Review* 21: 141–170.

10. Doucleff, M. 2018. "A lost secret: How to get kids to pay attention." All Things Considered broadcast. June 21, 2018. Transcript at: www.npr.org/sections/goatsandsoda/2018/06/21/621752789/a-lost-secret-how-to-get-kids-to-pay-attention.html (accessed February 16, 2019).

11. Based on a real case study, but made anonymous to protect the privacy of families and individuals.

12. Carey, B. 2018. "Walter Mischel, 88, psychologist famed for Marshmallow Test, dies." *The New York Times*. September 14, 2018.

13. Vaillant, G. 2012. *Triumphs of Experience: The Men of the Harvard Grant Study*. Cambridge, Mass: The Belknap Press of Harvard University Press, pp. 141–143.

14. Mindset Works (company website) https://www.mindsetworks.com/default (accessed January 5, 2019).

15. Simpson, J. 2004. *Touching the Void: The True Story of One Man's Miraculous Survival*, New York: Perennial, 218 pp.

16. Grice, E. 2011. Joe Simpson interview: "I'm not an easy person to be with." *The Telegraph*. October 15, 2011. https://www.telegraph.co.uk/lifestyle/8824399/Joe-Simpson-interview-Im-not-an-easy-person-to-be-with.html (accessed January 10, 2019).

Chapter 6

1. Linberg, L. D., Boggess, S., Porter, L., et al. 2000. "Teen risk-taking: A statistical portrait." Report prepared for the Urban Institute.

2. National Institute on Drug Abuse. 2018. "What are the long-term effects of heroin use?" https://www.drugabuse.gov/publications/research-reports/heroin/what-are-long-term-effects-heroin-use (accessed November 1, 2018).

3. Lorenz, T. 2018. "Teens are debating the news on Instagram." July 26, 2018. https://www.theatlantic.com/technology/archive/2018/07/the-instagram-forums-where-teens-go-to-debate-big-issues/566153/ (accessed on January 10, 2019).

4. Lorenz, T. 2019. "Teens are spamming Instagram to fight an apparent network of child porn." *The Atlantic*, January 8, 2019. https://www.the-atlantic.com/technology/archive/2019/01/meme-accounts-are-fighting-child-porn-instagram/579730/ (accessed January 10, 2019).

5. Sell, C. M. 1991. *Transitions Through Adult Life*. Grand Rapids: Zondervan.

6. Zinczenko, D. and Goulding, M. 2007. *Eat This, Not That!*. Pennsylvania: Rodale Books.

7. Hoffower, H. 2018. "Warren Buffett is the world's third-richest man—see how the notoriously frugal billionaire spends his fortune." *Business Insider*. October 13, 2018. https://www.businessinsider.com/how-warren-buffett-spends-net-worth-philanthropy-2018-10#he-previously-told-cnbc-and-yahoo-finances-off-the-cuff-that-hes-never-had-any-great-desire-to-have-multiple-houses-and-all-kinds-of-things-and-multiple-cars-3 (accessed November 1, 2018).

8. Buffett, W. 2010. "My philanthropic pledge." *CNN*. https://money.cnn.com/2010/06/15/news/newsmakers/Warren_Buffett_Pledge_Letter.fortune/index.htm (accessed January 5, 2019)

Chapter 7

1. Based on a real case study, but identifying details have been changed to protect the privacy of families and individuals.

2. Davis, J., Sinanis, M., and Colette, C. 2014. *Next Generation Success*. Cambridge, Mass: Cambridge Family Enterprise Press, 60 pp.

3. "America's richest families." *Forbes*. https://www.forbes.com/families/list/ (accessed November 1, 2018).

4. "Great American business leaders of the 20th century." Harvard Business School website. https://www.hbs.edu/leadership/20th-century-leaders/Pages/details.aspx?profile=whitney_macmillan (accessed November 1, 2018).

5. Orange, M. 2012. *Rothschild: Une banque au pouvoir*. Paris: Albin Michel, p. 10.

6. Das, A. 2013. "Inside the breakup of the Pritzker Empire." *Wall Street Journal*. November 26, 2013.

7. One such consultancy, serving both companies along with American Express, Deloitte, Du Pont, Kraft, General Motors and others, is Chicago-based Blair Miller Innovation, founded in 1990. Blair Miller Innovation (company website). 2019. http://www.blairmiller.com/clients.htm (accessed January 5, 2019).

8. Bosman, L. and Fernhaber, S. 2018. *Teaching the Entrepreneurial Mindset to Engineers*. New York: Springer.

9. Bort, J. 2013. "Reid Hoffman: Founding a startup is like 'throwing yourself off a cliff'." *Business Insider*. May 9, 2013. https://www.businessinsider.com/hoffman-linkedin-nearly-failed-2013-5 (accessed November 1, 2018).

10. Mortimer, J. 2003. "'Billy' was always the Ford to watch." *Automotive News*. June 16, 2003. http://www.autonews.com/article/20030616/SUB/306160805/billy-was-always-the-ford-to-watch (accessed November 1, 2018).

11. Swift, R. 2018. "Hermes keeps luxury in the family as it translates its model of super exclusivity online." *South China Morning Post*. April 3, 2018.

12. Evening Standard. 2009. "Another green Goldsmith—Ben, 28—aims to raise L150m and clean up." http://www.blairmiller.com/clients.htm (accessed January 5, 2019).

13. Chen, S. J. 2018. "Hong Kong's richest 2018: How a dying business was revived by focusing on happiness." *Forbes Asia*. February 2018.

14. Swidey, N. 2015. "Meet Boston's invisible billionaire." *Boston Globe*. May 3, 2015.

15. Based on a real case study, but made anonymous to protect the privacy of individuals.

16. Ward, M. 2016. "Warren Buffet's reading routine could make you smarter, science suggests." *CNBC*. https://www.cnbc.com/2016/11/16/warren-buffetts-reading-routine-could-make-you-smarter-suggests-science.html (accessed January 5, 2019).

17. Morris, C. 2009. *The Sages: Warren Buffett, George Soros, Paul Volcker, and the Maelstrom of Markets*. New York: PublicAffairs, 224 pp.

18. "Our story." World Bicycle Relief website. https://worldbicyclerelief.org/en/story/ (accessed November 1, 2018).

19. "December 2016 alumni of the month: Stanley R. Day Jr. '76 and Frederick K. Day '78." Hotchkiss website. December 1, 2016. https://www.hotchkiss.org/news/news-post-page/~post/december-2016-alumni-of-the-month-stanley-r-stan-day-jr-76-and-frederick-k-fk-day-78-20161116 (accessed November 1, 2018).

Chapter 8

1. McLeod, S. 2018. "Erik Erikson's stages of psychosocial development." *Simply Psychology* website. https://www.simplypsychology.org/Erik-Erikson.html (accessed November 1, 2018).

2. Davis, J. and Tagiuri, R. 1989. "The influence of life stage on father-son work relationships in family companies." *Family Business Review* 2(1): 47–74, March 1, 1989.

3. Sakoui, A. and Pfeiffer, T. "What's next in the battle for Rupert Murdoch's media empire." *Bloomberg.com.* July 13, 2018. https://www.bloomberg.com/news/articles/2018-07-13/what-s-next-in-the-battle-for-rupert-murdoch-s-media-empire (accessed September 6, 2018).

4. Tuccille, J. 2003. *Rupert Murdoch: Creator of a Worldwide Media Empire.* Frederick: Beard Books.

5. "17 next generation family enterprise leaders to watch in '17." Cambridge Family Enterprise Group website. https://cfeg.com/nextgenleaders2017/bio/mikkel-vestergaard-frandsen.html (accessed October 21, 2018).

6. Levy, G. 2013. "Rothschild versus Rothschild." *Dailymail.com.* https://www.dailymail.co.uk/news/article-2283192/Rothschild-versus-Rothschild-How-financial-genius-Nat-brought-earth-cousin.html (Accessed January 11, 2019).

7. Kapner, S. 2003. "Rothschild prepares for changing of guard." *The New York Times.* February 11, 2003. https://www.nytimes.com/2003/02/11/business/rothschild-prepares-for-changing-of-guard.html (accessed January 11, 2019).

8. Bain, D. 2012. "David de Rothschild: Banking on family ties." Campden FB. May 16, 2012. http://www.campdenfb.com/article/david-de-rothschild-banking-family-ties (accessed January 11, 2019).

9. Ibrahim, Y. M. 2016. "Restoring the house of Rothschild. 2018." *The New York Times.* October 27, 2016.

10. "Alfred Charles de Rothschild (1842-1918)." The Rothschild Archive. https://family.rothschildarchive.org/people/62-alfred-charles-de-rothschild-1842-1918 (accessed January 10, 2019)

11. "George Herbert, 5th Earl of Carnarvon." New World Encyclopedia. http://www.newworldencyclopedia.org/entry/George_Herbert,_5th_Earl_of_Carnarvon (accessed January 10, 2019).

12. "Arts, culture & libraries." The Rothschild Archive. https://www.rothschildarchive.org/family/philanthropy/arts_culture_libraries (accessed January 10, 2019).

13. Butrint Foundation (institutional website; archived). https://www.butrintfoundation.co.uk/services (accessed January 10, 2019).

14. Barry, C. "Plastiki sails into Sydney Harbour." *Australian Geographic.* July 27, 2010. https://www.webcitation.org/5vmIEKB1Z (accessed January 10, 2019).

Chapter 9

1. Sass, E. 2011. "2000–2010: The decade that killed (newspaper) classifieds." *MediaPost*. January 3, 2011. https://www.mediapost.com/publications/article/142129/2000-2010-the-decade-that-killed-newspaper-clas. html (accessed October 22, 2018).

2. Mitchell, B. 2005. *The Wall Street Journal* weekend edition: Expectations, surprises, disappointments. *Poynter*. September 21, 2005. http://www. poynter.org/content/content_view.asp?id=89351

3. Ellison, S. and Karnitschnig, M. 2007. "Murdoch wins his bid for Dow Jones." *Wall Street Journal*. August 1, 2007.

4. *The New York Times*. 1963. "Dow Jones shares will be marketed; DOW JONES STOCK TO BE MARKETED" May 2, 1963 p. B61 (archived by the New York Times Company and accessed on January 9, 2019).

5. Hill, C. 2007. Bancroft Cousin's letter: "Paying the price for our passivity." *Wall Street Journal*. July 27, 2007.

6. Klein, E. 2013. "Don Graham explains why he's selling *The Washington Post* to Jeff Bezos." *The Washington Post*. August 6, 2013.

7. Snyder, G. 2007. "Keeping up with the *Times*: The *New York Times* claws its way into the future." *Wired*. February 12, 2007. https://www.wired. com/2017/02/new-york-times-digital-journalism/ (accessed November 1, 2018).

8. Tran, K. 2017. "The New York Times soars past 3 million subscribers." *Business Insider*. December 7, 2018. https://www.businessinsider.com/ the-new-york-times-soars-past-3-million-subscribers-2017-12 (accessed January 6, 2019).

9. Peisner, J. 2018. "New York Times Co. reports $24 million profit, thanks to digital subscribers." *The New York Times*. August 8, 2018. https://www. nytimes.com/2018/08/08/business/media/new-york-times-earnings-subscriptions.html (accessed January 6, 2019).

10. Lee, E. 2016. "The *New York Times'* new boss-to-be literally wrote the plan to help it catch up in digital." *Recode*. October 19, 2016. https:// www.recode.net/2016/10/19/13329092/new-york-times-successor-ag-sulzberger (accessed November 1, 2018).

11. Snyder, G. ibid.

12. Galambos, L. and Abrahamson, E. J. 2002. *Anytime, Anywhere: Entrepreneurship and the Creation of a Wireless World*. New York: Cambridge University Press.

13. Aronsson, O. 2016. "Cristina Stenbeck in exclusive interview after stepping down as chairman at Kinnevik." *Breakit*. March 11, 2016. https://www.breakit.se/artikel/2996/cristina-stenbeck-in-exclusive-interview-after-stepping-down-as-chairman-at-kinnevik (accessed November 1, 2018).

14. "Ernesto Bertarelli profile." *Forbes*. https://www.forbes.com/profile/ernesto-bertarelli/#4d62ea6332d3 (accessed November 1, 2018).

15. Yohn, D. L. 2015. "How Levi's became a brand with staying power." *Entrepreneur*. April 2015.

16. Ibid.

Chapter 10

1. Shelley, P.B. Illus. Ott, J., 2015. *Ozymandias*, CreateSpace Independent Publishing Platform, 34 pp.

2. Honnold, A. 2018. "How I climbed a 3,000-foot vertical cliff—without ropes." *TED*.

3. Reiden, J. 2018. "Why Prince Harry and Meghan Markel's tour of Australia is Crucial to the future of the Monarchy." *Town & Country*. November 1, 2018.

Index

A.B. Kinnevik, 150, 151
Above-market compensation, 138
Active listening, 87
Adolescents, 11, 102, 108, 115
After-school job, for personal activities, 101
Agnelli family organization, 72, 73
Ainsworth, M., 91
Alibaba, 43
Antifragile, 2
AT&T, 48
Auchan, 28

Bertarelli, E., 153
Best school phenomenon, 113–114
Bezos, J., 146
Birman, Alexandre, 4–5, 81, 125, 158
Birman, Anderson, 5, 81
Boston Consulting Group, 47
Bowlby, J., 91
Brin, S., 63
Broadway, 50
Buffett, W., 112, 130
Business Insider, 53
Business leaders, xvi, xviii, xix, 25, 27, 48, 64, 65, 66, 67, 69, 80, 81, 89, 98, 111, 119, 124, 128, 136, 146, 150, 151
Butrint Foundation, 143

Cargill, 120
Centerprising, xxi, xxii, 4, 5, 21, 28, 36–39, 51, 63, 75, 81, 101, 113, 126, 129, 130, 151
    effective family organizational leader and, 72–73
    leadership traits, 64
Chan, G., 128
Chan, T.H., 128
Chief Capital Allocation Officer, 38
Child personalities, 97–98
China, 83, 123, 127
Chubb, 53
Churchill, W., 157
Collaborators and successful innovators, 4
Colson Corporation, 121
Concentric circles, of influence, 42–43
Cooper, G., 91
Corning, 54
    leadership and innovation culture and, 45–48
Craigslist, 145
Creating Shared Value concept, 82
Cultural sensitivity, 68
Curiosity and creative problem-solving, 114
Curse of Dichotomous Outcomes, 22

Dalmas, S., 12, 14
Davis, J., xxi, 7, 22, 25, 119, 135, 143
Day, FK, 131
Day brothers, 131
De Stäel, Madame, 10
Distributed systems, as fuzzier, 6–8
Dolnick, S., 148
Dow Chemical, 19
Dow Jones, 146
Drive (Pink), 80
Duke, D., 47, 48
Dumas, A., 124
Du Pont, E. I., 9, 10, 11, 57, 158
    and Quantum Machine, 10–19
Du Pont, P., 10–11, 12–13, 15, 17, 19, 58, 59, 158
Du Pont, S., 10–11, 155
Du Pont, V., 11–12, 13, 15, 17, 19
Du Pont de Nemours Père et Fils & Cie, 13
Dweck, C., 96

Early childhood, in learning core values, 98–100
Eat This, Not That! (Zinczenko and Goulding), 110
Edelman global survey (2014), 4
Edelman survey, 30
Edinburgh Festival Fringe, 49, 50
Edmond de Rothschild Group, 141
E.I. DuPont, 84
Elders and successors, clash between, 134–135
Eleutherian Mills, 18, 19, 20, 57
Elkann, J., xvii, 72–73
Empathy, 79, 86, 97, 110

Entrepreneur, xxi, 5, 6, 9, 10, 51, 52, 72, 98, 115, 117, 120, 129, 130, 137, 139, 140, 143, 151, 155
    profile of, 125–127
    social, 69, 70, 111
Entrepreneurial mindset, 121
Erikson, E., 133
Equality fallacy, 137–138
Exor, 72, 73

Fair treatment, issue of, 94
Family business, xvii, xx, xxi, 5, 6, 8, 14, 19, 22–25, 27, 28, 35, 45, 57, 72, 80, 80, 98, 103, 109, 117, 118, 124, 128, 129, 136–139, 141, 150, 153, 157
    evolution of, 32
Family ecosphere, xvii, 8, 9, 18, 19, 30–35, 36, 38, 39, 41–43, 51, 57, 59, 60, 61, 103, 119, 130, 137, 140, 143, 161
Family enterprise, 25–30; *see also individual entries*
    quantum impact multiplier, 42
Family leaders/leadership, xvi, xviii, 17, 22, 27, 28, 29, 31, 32–36, 65, 69, 78, 80, 84, 89, 92, 106, 107, 113, 118, 119, 123, 124, 128, 135, 138, 148, 152
Family organizations, evolution of, 21–22
    family business and, 22–25
    family ecosphere and, 30–35, 36, 37, 39–43
    family enterprise and, 25–30

Family owners/ownership, 7, 25, 48, 69, 119, 138, 140, 141, 145–148, 151–152, 154
Family sacrifice, 138–139
Family talent, 5
FANG (Facebook, Amazon, Netflix, Google), xv
Favored few compensation, 138
Ferguson, N., 40
Fiat, 72, 73
Fiber optics, 45, 46
Financial capital, 56, 110
  working with, 59–60
Fisk, J.B., 46
Forbes, 82
Ford, B., 123
Formal organization, 27
Founders, 77–78
Four Capitals, 30, 39, 55–59, 65, 72
Fourth Industrial Revolution, xix
Franklin, B., 11
Frazier-Hall, J., 58
Frictionless gearing, for quantum impact adaptation, 149–151
  for wealth creators and, 155
  being aligned and future-focused and, 145–149
  bringing authentic brand culture and, 153–155
  disruption scenario tackling and, 152–153
  vision sharing importance and, 151–152
Fringe theater, 50–51
Frugality, 99
Future-forward mindsets, 4–5, 34, 39, 72, 142, 149, 150, 152

intellectual capital and, 59
organizations designed for innovators and, 5–6
thinkers and experimenters with, 52–53

Gates, B., 63
Generational tensions, 77
  common ground with millennials and, 82–83
  individuality and, 79
  internal dictator and, 81
  internal drive and, 79–81
  resolving, 84
  second career and, 85–86
  spotting of stars and, 84–85
  success and failure and, 77–78
  vision alignment and, 83–84
Glueck study, 90, 94, 95, 133
Goldsmith, B., 125, 130
Good judgement, exercising, 74
Google, 63
Goulding, M., 110
Governance, evolution of, 41–42
Graham, D., 146
Graham, K., 147
Grant study, 89, 94, 117, 133
Guardian, The, 50
Gumber, A., 53

Hagley, 19
Hamilton, A., 16, 58
Hang Lung Group, 128
Harris Associates, 73
Hearst, W.R., III, 89
Hepburn, K., 45
Herbert, A., 142
Hermès, 125
Herro, D., 73

High performance, qualities
        with, 114
Hill, C., 146
Hill, T., 53
Hoffman, K., 91
Hoffman, R., xvii, 122
Honnold, A., 70, 160, 161
Houghton, A., 46, 47, 48, 52
Houghton, J., 54
House of Rothschild, The
        (Ferguson), 40
Human capital, 57
    non-family, 57
    working with, 60

IBM, 79, 83
I.E. du Pont de Nemours &
        Cie, 58
Incubation, of rising leaders,
        128–130
Incubators, 117
India, 123
Industrial Revolution, 9
Informal organization, 27
Innovation, xv, xx, 2, 6, 9, 10, 16,
        19, 22, 31, 34, 39, 45–50,
        59, 60, 61, 72, 82, 121, 126,
        129, 139, 147–152, 154,
        155, 161
Innovators, xv, xvi, xxi, 4, 5–6,
        9, 30, 38, 50, 51, 90, 150,
        158, 159
Intellectual capital, 59
    working with, 60
Intellectual property (IP), 47
Intentional consumption, 110
Interaction, with people in
        different micro-contexts,
        73–74
Intimacy, as indicator of
        longevity, 90

Intrapreneur, 9, 120, 128, 129,
        136, 155
    profile of, 122
        explorer, 124–125
        insider, 122–124
IP, *see* Intellectual property (IP)

Jacob, Lord Rothschild, 41
Jefferson, T., 11, 13, 14, 17, 19,
        57, 58
Jobs, S., 63

Kalanick, T., 66–67
Keenan, J., 53
Kevlar, 59

Leadership traits, exceptional,
        63–64
    centerpriser and, 72–73
    centerprising, 64
    challenges, 64–65
        governance roles, 66–67
        mandate to lead, 65–66
        versatility and cultural
            sensitivity, 67–68
    measurement of, 74–75
    qualities of, 73–74
    types of, 68–70
        performance versus
            success, 70–72
Lee, B., xv
Lee, S., 3, 126
Lee Kum Kee, 3, 126
Levi Strauss, 152, 154
LifeStraw, 139
Livingston, R., 58
LKK Health Products Group
        Ltd, 126
Longevity DNA, 3–4, 32, 41, 45,
        50, 66, 136, 158
    of Amo Houghton, 48–49

child personalities and,
        97–98
Corning leadership and
        innovation culture and,
        45–48
early childhood in core
        values learning, 98–100
leadership development from
        birth and, 90–91
    parental engagement,
        92–93
    secure attachment, 91–92
    strong moral core
        formation, 92
marshmallow test and, 95
rising generation's burden
        and, 93–94
work ethic and growth
        mindset and, 96–97
Lucy, C., 46–47
Lycra, 59

MacMillan, W., 120
Marginalized talent, 6
Marmon Holdings, 121
Marshmallow test, 95
Mischel, W., 95
Mitterand, F., xvii, 120
Money, significance of, 110–111,
        143
Morris, C., 130
Mothership, 32–33, 38
Mulliez, 28, 141
Murdoch, R., 135, 136, 146, 150
Musk, E., 52, 53

Nasser, J., 123
Neo-Confucians, 42
Neoprene, 59
New Digital Age, xv, xx, 4, 8, 9,
        30, 148

News Corp Australia, 136
News Corporation, 146
Newsweek, 147
New York Times, The, 7, 141, 147,
        148, 153
New York Times Company,
        The, 148
    innovation cultural and
        attributes of, 148–149
Non-family companies, 30
N.M. Rothschild & Sons, 142

Organization-focused
        approach, 28, 30
Ozymandias (Shelley), 158

Page, L., 63
Parental engagement, 92–93
Parenting, *see* Teens
Passion, harnessing,
        130–131
Passive owners, 143
People-focused approach, 28
PermaNet, 139
Perpich, D., 148
Pew Research Center, 82
Pink, D., 80
Porter, M., 82
Portfolio builder, 121
    profile of, 127–128
Powell, B., 91
Practical futurism, 53–55
Pritzker, J., 121
Productive outlook, on
        goals, 114
Psychological development
        theory, 133
    intimacy versus isolation
        stage, 133
    nesting phase, 133
    young family phase, 134

Quantum Machine, 8–9, 33,
     35–36
  of British Theater, 49–51
  centerprising and, 36–39
  du Pont and, 10–19
  with four capitals, 59–61

Raising a Secure Child (Hoffman,
     Cooper, and Powell), 91
Resilience, xvi, 97, 114
Rising leaders; *see also individual*
     entries
  skills for, 86–87
RIT, *see* Rothschild Investment
     Trust (RIT)
RIT Capital Partners, 141
Rockefeller, D., 41, 141
Rockefeller, J.D., Jr., 60
Rockefeller Center, 60
Rockefeller Financial Services,
     41, 141
Rothschild, A.C. de, 142
Rothschild, B de, 141
Rothschild, D.M. de, 143
Rothschild, D.R de, xvii, 120, 141
Rothschild, E. de, 140, 141
Rothschild, J., 140, 141, 143
Rothschild, M.A., 39
Rothschild Archive, The, 41
Rothschild Family, five arrows
     of, 39–41
Rothschild Investment Trust
     (RIT), 41, 141

Schutz, 5
Seasoned leaders, xx, 21, 34, 36,
     38, 66, 78, 79, 81, 84, 85,
     87, 128, 157–161
Second career, 85–86
Secure attachment, 91–92
Self-awareness, 3, 74, 93, 115

Self-control, 95, 97, 100
Self-governance, 66
Self-regulation, xix
Senior leaders, xxi, 2, 3, 4, 43, 55,
     79, 122, 124, 134, 135, 139,
     140, 158, 160
Sensitivity, developing, 74
Serono, 153
Shelley, P.B., 158
Siemens, 46
Simpson, J., 99
Skill sets, meaning and
     significance of, 70
Slim, C., 147
Social capital, 58–59
  working with, 60–61
Social contract, 64, 65
Social entrepreneurs, 69, 70
SpaceX, 52
SRAM, 131
Stenbeck, C., 150
Stenbeck, J., 150
Strong moral core
     formation, 92
Successful entry, into family
     enterprise, 136
  and wealth creators
     compensation package
        structuring for, 137–139
     flexible roles for, 136
     positions to aspire, 136–137
Succession planning, 23, 25
Sulzberger, A.G., 147, 148
Sweat equity, 57

Taguiri, R., 22
Taleb, N.N., 2
Talent incubators, 38
Tech research today, 45
Teens, 101–104
  proactive parenting strategies

best school phenomenon, 113–114

effective leadership traits in teens, 114–116

family identity, 107–109

helping teen building friendship circle, 104–105

money talk with teens, 109–113

showing up at teens' performances and games, 105–106

spending time with teen, 104

teens in choosing tribe, 106

trusted advisors building, 107

Teflon, 59

Telegraph, The, 99

Tencent, 43

Three-Circle Model, 23–25, 28

Three Generation Curse, The, 22

Times, The, 148

Touching the Void (Simpson), 99

Toussard, L., 14

Traits, meaning and significance of, 70

Transformation, 2–3

Uber, 67

Uncertainty, dealing with, 114

United Nations, 53

Vaillant, G., 90

Vanderbilt, B., 85

Vanderbilt, C., 85

Vestergaard, 82

Vestergaard, M., 139,

Vestergaard, T., 139

Vestergaard Frandsen, 82,

Vestergaard-Frandsen, M., 82

Vision alignment process, 83–84

Wall Street Journal, The, 146, 147, 152

Washington Post, The, 146, 147

Watson, Thomas, Jr., 79, 83, 84, 150

Wealth creators

abundance, to lead Rothschild, 140–144

adaptation for, 155–156

compensation package structuring for, 137–139

and equity upside, 139–140

flexible roles for, 136

mindset of, 121–122

positions to aspire, 136–137

types of, 119–121

West End productions, 50

Weymouth, K., 147

WHEB, 125

Winner-take-all mentality, xviii

Wired magazine, 7

Work ethic and growth mindset, 96–97

World Bicycle Relief, 131

Young adults, 118–119

ZeroFly, 139

Zinczenko, D., 110

For Product Safety Concerns and Information please contact our EU
representative GPSR@taylorandfrancis.com
Taylor & Francis Verlag GmbH, Kaufingerstraße 24, 80331 München, Germany